73-45

Introducing the Holy Land

Introducing
the Holy Land

A Guidebook for First-Time Visitors

by J. Maxwell Miller

Mercer University Press
Macon, Ga. 31207

ISBN 0-86554-034-9

All books published by Mercer University Press are produced
on acid-free paper which exceeds the minimum standards set by the
National Historical Publications and Records Commission.

Library of Congress Cataloging in Publication Data

Miller, James Maxwell, 1937—
    Introducing the Holy Land.

    Includes bibliographies and index.
    1. Palestine—Description and travel—Guide-books.
    2. Jordan—Description and travel—Guide-books.
        I. Title.

DS103.M54   1982   915.694'0454   82-14424
ISBN 0-86554-034-9

Contents

Part Three

For Further Reference

Index

Foreword

It is my pleasure each summer to conduct a tour of Jordan, Israel, and Greece for twenty carefully selected seminary students and laypersons. Five outstanding students are chosen each time from Candler School of Theology of Emory University, five from Columbia Theological Seminary, five from the Southern Baptist Theological Seminary in Louisville, Kentucky, and five laypersons from positions of leadership in business, industry, and the professions. This guidebook was prepared originally for the private use of the travel group and has gone through several editions—each new edition expanded in the light of new questions which arose during the process of the previous year's tour.

I wish to express my deep appreciation to those who were instrumental in establishing the travel program, to the private foundation which provides the necessary funding, and to all of those who, while participating in the program, have shared in the authorship of this book. Beth Parker served as photography editor and supplied most of the photographs. The photograph of the Mesha Inscription (page 26) was provided by the Louvre. The photograph of excavations at et-Tell (page 28) was supplied by J. A. Callaway, who directed these excavations.

—J. Maxwell Miller

*Dedicated to Pollard Turman,
participant in the first tour,
whose strength and spirit
set the tone of the program.*

Preface

This guidebook is designed primarily for first-time visitors to the Holy Land who want to make the most of their visit but do not have time for extensive reading in advance. My intention has been to provide a brief overview of the geography and history of the land, and to support this with maps, archaeological plans and chronological outlines which can be consulted from time to time as the need arises. While the emphasis of the guidebook is on biblical times and places, I have been concerned to present the Holy Land in its broader geographical context, the "Fertile Crescent," and to take into account the whole sweep of Middle Eastern history and culture. Certainly any visitor to the Middle East should know something about the Crusades, for example, and have some understanding of the events which led to the current Arab-Israeli conflict.

My use of the term "Holy Land" throughout this guidebook is not intended to ignore present-day political realities, but to facilitate an overview of the geography of the area and the continuity of its history through the ages. Specifically, I use the term Holy Land to refer to that portion of the eastern Mediterranean seaboard south of the Lebanon and Anti-Lebanon Mountains, bounded on the west by the Mediterranean Sea, on the east by the Arabian Desert and on the south by the Sinai Desert. In terms of present-day political boundaries, the Holy Land corresponds to the Hashemite Kingdom of Jordan, Israel, and certain territories under Israeli military control (Gaza Strip, West Bank, Gholan Heights).

The guidebook has three parts: Part I provides general orientation, beginning with an overview of the "Fertile Crescent" and a brief sketch of the whole long sweep of Middle Eastern history. The emphasis here is on the overall picture rather than on the details. It is suggested that one might read this first part of the guidebook before the trip or on the flight over. Part II focuses on the actual places which tourists normally visit in the Holy Land, or should visit, and summarizes basic historical and archaeological information about each site. Designed for use during the tour, this second section of the guidebook is illustrated with simplified road maps, site plans and excerpts from ancient documents. Part III is packed with details—a more thorough survey of the history of the Holy Land with maps and chronological charts, a glossary of geographical terms, and the like—the sort of information a serious traveler in the Holy Land needs at his fingertips. This last section is intended more for reference than for general reading, but it should be especially useful after the tour is over.

As indicated above, the guidebook is designed primarily for visitors to the Holy Land. I have tried to write it in such a fashion, however, that it will be useful to "armchair travelers" as well—or to anyone for that matter who is interested in the geography, history and archaeology of the land of the Bible. But remember, it is intended as a beginner's introduction. Also it focuses on the "highlights," the main points of interest which, in my opinion, deserve first attention by travelers who have only a limited time to spend in the Holy Land. For those who have occasion to explore the land more thoroughly and wish to do so at a more advanced level, I have included "Suggestions for Further Reading" at the end.

Part One

Background Information

The Holy Land in Context

The Fertile Crescent, Cradle of Western Civilization. The Holy Land represents the southwestern end of a curved strip of cultivable land which historians often refer to as the "Fertile Crescent." Specifically, the Fertile Crescent consists of the Eastern Mediterranean Seaboard and the Tigris-Euphrates river valley. One is tempted to think of the Nile as an extension of the Fertile Crescent since its river valley is extremely fertile and also played a major role in man's most ancient history. Egypt's cultural traditions were rather different from those of its Fertile Crescent neighbors in ancient times, however, and the Sinai Desert tended to isolate Egypt from them.

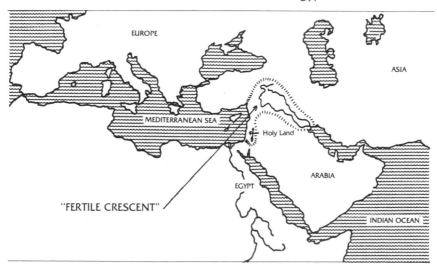

Map 1: THE HOLY LAND, SOUTHWESTERN END OF THE "FERTILE CRESCENT"

The following are some key names and geographical terms associated with the Fertile Crescent during ancient times.

Mesopotamia

"Between the Rivers" in Greek, this name refers to the eastern horn of the Fertile Crescent, drained by the Tigris and Euphrates Rivers. Mesopotamia was the homeland of the Sumerians, Babylonians and Assyrians.

Babylonia

The Southeastern portion of Mesopotamia, nearest the Persian Gulf, is known in the Bible as the "Land of Shinar" (Gen. 10:10). This was the home of the Sumerians who provided us with our earliest written records. Ur (possibly the Ur associated with Abraham) was one of the old Sumerian city-states. Southern Mesopotamia is usually referred to as Babylonia, after Babylon, which emerged as the dominant city-state in that area after the decline of Sumerian civilization.

On two different occasions rulers of Babylon were able to establish empires involving virtually all of the Fertile Crescent. The first instance was during the reign of Hammurabi (approximately 1750 B.C.); the next instance, during the seventh and sixth centuries B.C., occasioned the "Babylonian Exile" of the Jews.

Assyria

The people who lived further north along the banks of the Tigris River and two of its tributaries, the Greater Zab and the Lesser Zab, were known as Assyrians. Their major city was Ashur, from which their name is derived. The Assyrian empire reached its zenith during the ninth through the seventh centuries B.C. when they dominated all the kingdoms of the Fertile Crescent, including Israel and Judah. Successively, Ashur, Calah and Nineveh served as capitals of the Assyrian empire. Jonah was sent to Nineveh. The book of Nahum celebrates its fall.

Aram/Syria

The territory drained by the upper Euphrates, along with the area extending southward as far as Damascus, was called Aram in ancient times. Later called Syria by the Greek and Roman geographers, Aram is normally translated "Syria" in the old Greek and English translations of the Bible. Note that "Syria" and "Assyria" are not the same. Among the prominent Aramean (Syrian) city-states were Haran, Carchemish, Hamath and Damascus.

Phoenicia

The Phoenicians occupied the shores of the Mediterranean Sea
west of Aram. Separated from the hinterland by the Lebanon and
Anti-Lebanon mountains, the Phoenician cities, including Byblos, Tyre and Sidon, were actively engaged in maritime trade.
Often in competition with each other, these great cities established colonies throughout the Mediterranean, one of the most
famous being Carthage in North Africa.

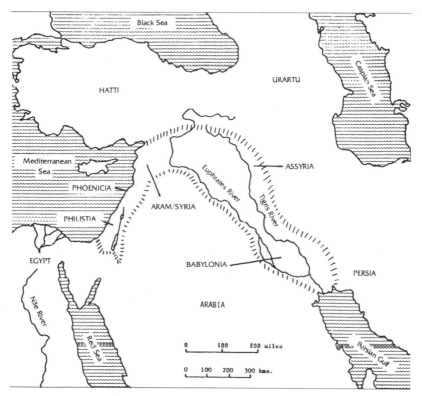

Map 2: THE "FERTILE CRESCENT"

Hatti/Anatolia

Hatti, in the heartland of Asia Minor, was the land of the Hittites,
rivals of the Egyptians, Assyrians and Babylonians during the
seventeenth through the thirteenth centuries B.C. Greeks colo-
nized the western shores of Asia Minor and called it Anatolia. The
kingdom of Lydia, whose best known king was Croesus ("rich as

Croesus"), flourished in southwestern Asia Minor during the seventh and sixth centuries B.C.

Arabia

The Fertile Crescent curves around the northwestern corner of the Arabian Peninsula, the interior of which is a vast desert. The settled occupation of Arabia has always been primarily along the western coast (along the Red Sea) and in the southwestern corner. The latter area, termed Arabia Felix ("Arabia the Fortunate") by classical geographers, produced frankincense and myrrh trees, a source of perfumes and incense. This may have been the biblical land of Sheba (see especially 1 Kings 10).

Sinai

The Sinai peninsula at the northern end of the Red Sea, was considered a part of ancient Egypt. It served as a land bridge between Egypt and the Fertile Crescent proper. But because of Sinai's hot, dry and poorly policed condition, travelers and merchants usually preferred to sail along the Mediterranean coast between Phoenicia and the Nile delta. This was a three- or four-day trip, contrasting with the minimum of seven or eight days overland.

Persia

The Elamites, Medes and Persians occupied the mountains and plateaus east of Mesopotamia; their major cities were Susa, Ecbatana and Persepolis respectively. Persia emerged as the dominant power in the Fertile Crescent during the sixth through the fourth centuries B.C., even conquering Egypt and threatening the Greek city-states. Cyrus the Great of Persia (538-529 B.C.) receives the credit for allowing the Jewish exiles to return to their homeland.

Urartu/Ararat

The mountainous territory northeast of the Fertile Crescent, around Lake Van, is called Urartu in the early Assyrian records and Ararat in the Old Testament (Gen. 8:4). Recent attempts to discover remains of Noah's Ark focus on this area.

Philistia

The territory south of the Lebanon and Anti-Lebanon mountains was called "Philistia" (literally "the land of the Philistines") by the Greek and Roman geographers. Palestine is the English pronunciation of Philistia. Actually the Philistines lived only along the coastal plain.

Travelers in the Middle East often are surprised that distances between points of interest seem so short. "As the crow flies," Jerusalem is only about 200 miles from Cairo, hardly more than half that distance from Damascus, and approximately 550 miles from Baghdad, near ancient Babylon. But it must be understood that travel and communication were much less efficient in ancient times than today. In fact, one cannot go "as the crow flies" even today because of political barriers.

The Long Sweep of History. In addition to being a part of the Fertile Crescent, The Holy Land serves as a land bridge between continents—Europe, Asia, and Africa. Consequently it has always played a crucial role in human history. The history of the Holy Land can be confusing to Westerners if for no other reason than the sheer length of time involved and the prevalence of unusual and unfamiliar names. Nevertheless, the traveler who has even a general grasp of the main historical features will benefit much more from a visit to the Holy Land than those who do not.

As an aid to basic understanding it is useful to divide the long sweep of Middle Eastern history into eleven major periods. Only approximate dates can be established for the earliest periods. The abbreviation "ca.," for Latin "circa," means "approximately."

Outline of Periods

Prehistoric times (Stone Age)	before ca. 3200 B.C.
Bronze Age	ca. 3200-1200 B.C.
Iron Age	ca. 1200-333 B.C.
Hellenistic Period	333-64 B.C.
Roman Period	64 B.C.-A.D. 324
Byzantine Period	A.D. 324-640
Early Arab Period	A.D. 640-1099
Crusader Period	A.D. 1099-1260
Mamluk Period	A.D. 1260-1517
Ottoman Period	A.D. 1517-1918
Mandate Period and following	A.D. 1918-

A brief description of each of these periods is provided below. For a more detailed outline of the archaeological periods and the history of the Holy Land during each period, see Part Three below, "History of the Holy Land in Outline."

Mount Carmel Caves, where human and artifactual remains
from the Paleolithic Period have been discovered

• *Prehistoric times* (pre-ca. 3200 B.C.). There is archaeological evidence of human occupation in the Middle East dating at least as early as ca. 300,000 years ago, and probably much earlier. Our oldest written records extend back no earlier than ca. 3200 B.C., when the first true cities began to emerge. This long period of time when people were living in the Middle East but did not have any written records is often referred to as "prehistoric times." Archaeologists call it the "Stone Age," subdividing it into the Paleolithic (Old Stone) Period, the Mesolithic (Middle Stone) Period, the Neolithic (New Stone) Period and the Chalcolithic (Copper-Stone) Period.

• *Bronze Age* (ca. 3200-1200 B.C.). Small villages already existed during the Neolithic Period—Jericho was one of these. Major fortified cities began to emerge ca. 3200 B.C., representing a significant new development: true urban centers. These cities flourished for the next 2,000 years, typically as independent city-states, but united from time to time into kingdoms and empires. This approximately 2,000 year period is known as the "Bronze Age," and in many respects it represents the height of cultural achievement in the Middle East. It was the inhabitants of these most ancient cities who developed writing. This was the age of the great pharaohs and of the old Babylonian and Hittite empires.

The end of the Bronze Age was a turbulent time for the nations of the ancient Middle East. The Hittite Empire collapsed, possibly due to pressure from the "Sea Peoples" mentioned in Egyptian documents. Egypt survived the onslaughts of the Sea Peoples but ceased to dominate international affairs. Most present day biblical scholars date the Hebrew exodus from Egypt at the end of this age, late thirteenth century B.C. A victory inscription of Merneptah, an Egyptian pharaoh who reigned ca. 1236-1223 B.C., provides the earliest non-biblical reference to "Israel." See below, under "Deciphering Ancient Languages," for a translation of the crucial lines of Merneptah's inscription.

Asiatic captive as depicted in an Egyptian Inscription from the Late Bronze Age.

• *Iron Age* (ca. 1200-333 B.C.). The cultural traditions established in the Fertile Crescent and Egypt during the Bronze Age continued for yet another 1,000 years without radical change. Clearly the golden age had passed, especially for Egypt. In the early centuries of the Iron Age a number of small local kingdoms emerged in all parts of the Fertile Crescent. Eventually these minor kingdoms fell under the influence of a succession of larger, eastern-based empires—Assyria, Babylon and Persia, each in turn.

The Iron Age roughly corresponds to Old Testament times. Among the small kingdoms which appeared during the early centuries of the age were Israel, Edom, Moab, Ammon and a league of Philistine cities. Israel was divided into two separate kingdoms after Solomon's death (ca. 925 B.C.). The northern Israelite kingdom, still called Israel, was destroyed by the Assyrians in 722 B.C. (2 Kings 17). The southern Israelite kingdom, called Judah, was destroyed by the Babylonians in 586 B.C., and many of its leaders exiled (2 Kings 25). Under Persian rule the exiles were allowed to return (Ezra 1).

• *Hellenistic Period* (333-64 B.C.). Alexander the Great invaded the Middle East, defeating Persia in 333 B.C. This marked the end of the old order and introduced a new age; Middle Eastern history and culture would now be bound more closely to Greece and Rome. The Greeks referred to themselves as "Hellenes," and historians use the term "Hellenistic" to refer to their culture.

After Alexander's death, his empire was divided and ruled by his top military officials. Two of these officials, Ptolemy and Seleucus, gained control of the Middle East at that time. Ptolemy ruled Egypt and founded a dynasty which remained in power there until 31 B.C. Cleopatra was the last of the Ptolemaic rulers. Seleucus ruled Mesopotamia and Syria, founding the Seleucid dynasty which remained in power until defeated by Pompey in 64 B.C.

The Holy Land fell first to the Ptolemys (312-200 B.C.) and then to the Seleucids (200-166 B.C.). In 166 B.C. the Jews rebelled against Antiochus IV, one of the Seleucid rulers, and established an independent kingdom in Jerusalem. This was the so-called "Maccabean rebellion" (see the Inter-Testamental books of 1-2 Maccabees). Jewish rulers who followed are known as the "Maccabean" or "Hasmonean" rulers. Hasmonean kings conquered virtually all of the Holy Land and forcibly converted much of its population to Judaism.

"Herodian" lamp, typical oil lamp used in the Holy Land at the end of the Hellenistic period and the beginning of the Roman period.

• *Roman Period* (64 B.C.-A.D. 324). In 64 B.C. Pompey annihilated the Seleucid kingdom and in its place created the Roman province of Syria. The following year he marched on Jerusalem to settle a squabble between two contenders for the Hasmonean throne, Aristobolus II and Hyrcanus II. After this, and for the next two and a half centuries, Rome dictated *who* would rule *what* parts of the Holy Land, for *how long*. Surely the most famous Rome-appointed ruler was Herod the Great (37-4 B.C.). Jesus' ministry and the beginnings of Christianity belong to the first century A.D., in the aftermath of Herod the Great's spectacular reign. There were two major Jewish revolts—A.D. 66-70 and 132-135—both crushed ruthlessly by the Romans. Eventually the Holy Land was incorporated into the Roman province system and became an integral component of the Roman empire. The majority of the population worshiped the pagan gods; the exceptions were the surviving Jewish and Samaritan communities, mostly in Galilee, and the Christian movement, rapidly growing though still "underground."

• *Byzantine Period* (A.D. 324-640). The Byzantine period represents a continuation of the cultural traditions of the Hellenistic and Roman periods, but with two distinctively new developments: (1) By the early fourth century the Roman empire had become divided into two different realms—the west, which looked to Rome for leadership, and the east, which looked to Byzantium. The peoples of the Middle East looked to Byzantium. (2) Christianity became the official religion of the Roman/Byzantine world. The years A.D. 324-25 are significant dates: Constantine emerged as sole ruler of the Roman empire in 324 and made Byzantium his capital, renaming it Constantinople. The following year he presided over the first officially sanctioned convocation of Christian churches. This was the Council of Nicea, convened in a town of that same name near Constantinople.

For the next three centuries the Holy Land remained relatively secure within the Byzantine realm. Churches replaced pagan temples throughout the land; population increased to an all time high; Caesarea became the major economical and political center.

Dome of the rock, architecture from the Early Arab Period

- *Early Arab Period* (A.D. 640-1099). A Persian invasion of Syria-Palestine in A.D. 611-614 forewarned of a weakened Byzantium. Heraclius, the Byzantine emperor, was able to expell the Persians in 628, but by 640 most of Egypt, the Holy Land, and Syria had fallen into Muslim hands. The first major Muslim victory in the Holy Land occurred near the Yarmuk River in 636. Jerusalem fell to Caliph Omar in 637.

The Hellenistic-Roman-Byzantine periods had represented essentially a cultural continuum. Now the Middle East was in for a more radical change. Arab culture began to take hold, and with it, Islam. After the first four Caliphs who ruled from Medina, the so-called "Rightly Guided Caliphs," the Holy Land was dominated in turn by the Umayyad caliphs who ruled from Damascus (661-750), and Abbasid caliphs who ruled from Baghdad (750-969) and the Fatimid caliphs who ruled from Cairo (969-1171).

- *Crusader Period* (A.D. 1099-1260). Seljuk Turks from central Asia invaded Mesopotamia and took Damascus in 1055. By 1077 they conquered Jerusalem. It was primarily in response to this Seljuk conquest of the Holy Land and their disruption of Christian pilgrim routes that the Crusades were launched. As a result of the First Crusade (1097-1099), four Latin kingdoms were established: Edessa, Antioch, Tripoli, Jerusalem. These were modeled after Middle Age European kingdoms, castles and all. The Latin kingdom of Jerusalem existed for almost a hundred years (1099-1187).

This first phase of the Crusader period ended in 1187 when Saladin crushed the Crusader army at the "Horns of Hattin." By the end of that same year virtually all of the Crusader castles, including Jerusalem, had fallen to Saladin. The Crusaders were able to maintain a foothold in the Holy Land, mostly along the coast, for another hundred years; but their attempts to recover Jerusalem were never entirely successful.

- *Mamluk Period* (A.D. 1260-1517). The Fatamid caliphs of Egypt were displaced by the Ayyubids, Saladin's dynasty, in 1171. After Saladin's death, the Ayyubids increasingly delegated their authority through slaves of foreign birth purchased as children and educated in the royal court. These slave-administrators were known as Mamluks and soon became the real masters of Egypt.

A Mongol invasion was halted by the Mamluks in 1260 with a decisive battle at Ain Jalud in the Jezreel Valley. Baybars, who commanded the Mamluk army, proclaimed himself sultan of Egypt in 1260. He and the next two sultans of his line (Qalawun and el-Ashraf Khalil) systematically reduced the remaining Crusader castles, expelled the Crusaders from the Holy Land, and followed a "scorched earth" policy along the coast to prevent their return.

For the next two and a quarter centuries the Holy Land was in Mamluk hands. These were exceedingly difficult years for the local population; the Mamluks were harsh rulers, officially condoning exploitation of their subjects.

* *Ottoman Period* (A.D. 1517-1918). A horde of Ottoman Turks entered Asia Minor ca. 1300. In 1353 they bypassed Constantinople, crossed the Dardanelles, and soon were threatening even Vienna. Finally, in 1453, Constantinople also fell to them. Constantinople represented the last surviving remnant of the old Byzantine empire; the Turks renamed it Istanbul and made it their capital. A clash between the Turks and Mamluks was inevitable. The decisive battle occurred near Aleppo in 1516, the Turks victorious. By the following year the Holy Land and Egypt were in Ottoman hands.

The Turkish empire reached its zenith in the sixteenth century, especially during the reign of Suleiman the "Magnificent" (1520-1566). Soon after, the empire began its decline. The Turks lost extensive territories in the nineteenth century, although most of the Middle East remained at least nominally in Ottoman hands until World War I.

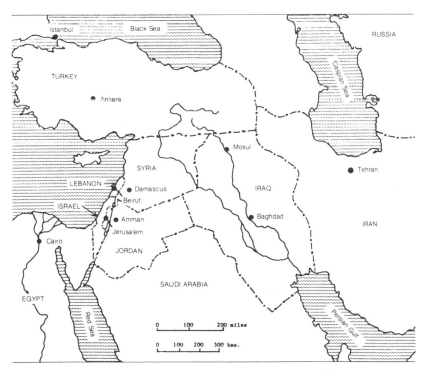

Map 3: PRESENT-DAY BOUNDARIES OF THE MIDDLE EASTERN COUNTRIES

• *Mandate Period and Following* (1918-   ). After World War I, most of the former Ottoman territorial possessions in the Middle East were assigned to France and England as "mandates." France received Syria, including present-day Lebanon; England received Mesopotamia and the Holy Land. The Holy Land was divided into two parts. The area west of the Jordan River was designated "Palestine" and administered directly by the British. The area east of Jordan was established as an emirate (kingdom) under British protection. At the beginning of World War I Britain had declared Egypt a protectorate. England maintained a presence there until World War II, although the protectorate status was officially terminated in 1922.

The Middle East is divided into independent nations today, each with a unique history of struggle. Compare Map 2 of the Fertile Crescent, above, with Map 3 which shows present-day boundaries. Note that ancient Persia corresponds inexactly to present-day Iran; ancient Babylonia and Assyria are within modern Iraq; ancient Phoencia approximates today's Lebanon. A crucial new development since World War II is the rise of modern Israel.

Rediscovering
the Ancient World

Essentially the kingdoms and empires of the ancient Middle East have been rediscovered during modern times. The following is a sampling of the highlights of this rediscovery.

Early travelers. Contact between Europe and the Middle East was radically diminished following the Crusaders' expulsion; this situation continued during the Mamluk and early Ottoman periods. There were occasional European visitors to the Mamluk and Ottoman realms, including a trickle of Christian and Jewish pilgrims to the Holy Land, but travel was difficult and dangerous. Usually these early travelers did not venture beyond the main cities and roads.

Felix Fabri. One pilgrim of the Mamluk period was Brother Felix Fabri, a German dominican. Brother Fabri made two trips to Jerusalem, in 1480 and 1483 (Columbus was raising funds for his proposed westward voyage to India). On the second trip he served as chaplain and "tour host" for a small group of his countrymen. They arrived in Venice in April and negotiated with a ship captain for what amounted to a round-trip packaged tour. The captain was approved by Venetian authorities for the venture, his ship a "three-banked galley large and broad, and besides this, new and clean." A twenty-three article contract was drawn up that included the following provisions:

§ The captain shall take us pilgrims from Venice to Joppa and bring us back to Venice.

§ He shall properly provide a galley with experienced mariners, and shall have on board a sufficient armament for defense of the galley from attacks of pirates and enemies.

§ The captain shall be bound to provide the pilgrims with a sufficiency of good bread and biscuit, good wine and sweet water, freshly put on board with meat, eggs, and other eatables of the same sort.

§ The captain shall be bound to protect the pilgrims, both in the galley and out of it, from being attacked or ill-used by the galley-slaves. . . . He shall also be bound to prevent the slaves from molesting them on land, as far as he is able, and he shall not place any article in the pilgrims' berths.

§ The captain shall let the pilgrims remain in the Holy Land for the due length of time, and shall not hurry them too fast, and shall lead them to the usual places and go with them in person. We especially wish him to raise no objections to leading them to the Jordan, which pilgrims always find a difficulty in doing, and he shall save them from all troubles with the infidels.

§ All dues, all money for safe-conduct, and for passes and other expenses, in whatever names they may be charged, or in whatever place they have to be paid, shall be paid in full by the captain alone on behalf of all pilgrims without their being charged anything, and he shall likewise pay the great fees; the smaller fees we will see to ourselves.

§ In return for all these expenses to be incurred and things to be done by the captain, each pilgrim shall be bound to pay 40 ducats, newly minted. However, the pilgrim shall pay one-half of this sum in Venice, and the remainder in Joppa. . .

§ The captain shall assign to the pilgrims some convenient place on board of the galley for keeping chickens or fowls, and his cooks shall permit the pilgrims' cooks to use their fire for cooking for the pilgrims at their pleasure.

§ Should any pilgrim on board of the galley happen to fall so ill that he cannot remain in the stench of the cabin, the captain shall be bound to give such a person some place to rest in on the upper deck. . . .

Brother Fabri and his group arrived in Joppa on July 2, 1483. They were obliged to wait on board their ship for three days until a representative of the Franciscan order, which maintained the Christian holy places in Jerusalem, arrived with safe-conduct papers. The journey from Joppa to Jerusalem, under heavy Saracen guard, took three more days. They camped at Ramla the first night (near present-day Tel Aviv airport) and were given guidelines for pilgrim behavior. These were read aloud in Latin and German. Among the guidelines were:

§ No pilgrim ought to wander alone about the holy places without a Saracen guide, because this is dangerous and unsafe. . . .

§ The pilgrim should beware of stepping over the sepulchers of the Saracens because they are greatly vexed when they see this done, and pelt with stones anyone who steps over them. . . .

§ Should any pilgrim be struck by a Saracen, however unjustly, he must not return the blow. . . .

§ Let the pilgrim beware of chipping off fragments from the Holy Sepulchre, and from the buildings at other places, and spoiling the hewn stones. . . .

§ Pilgrims of noble birth must not deface walls by drawing their coats-of-arms thereon, or by writing their names. . .for such conduct gives great offense to the Saracens, and they think those who do so to be fools. . . .

§ Pilgrims must beware of laughing together as they walk about Jerusalem to see the holy places, but they must be grave and devout, both on account of the holy places, and of the example which they afford to the infidels, and also lest the latter should suspect that we are laughing at them, which annoys them exceedingly. They are always suspicious about laughter and merriment among pilgrims.

§ Let the pilgrim beware of gazing upon any woman whom they meet, because all Saracens are exceedingly jealous and a pilgrim may in ignorance run himself into danger through the fury of some jealous husband.

§ Should any woman beckon to a pilgrim or invite him by signs to enter a house, let him on no account do so, because the woman does this treacherously at the instigation of some men, in order that the Christian when he enters may be robbed, and perhaps slain. Those who are not careful in these matters incur great danger.

§ Let every pilgrim beware of giving a Saracen wine when he asks for drink, whether on the roadside or elsewhere, because straightway after one single draught thereof he becomes mad and the first man whom he attacks is the pilgrim who gave it to him.

§ Let every pilgrim carefully guard his own property, and never leave it lying about any place where the Saracens are, otherwise it will straightway vanish, whatever it may be. . . .

§ Let no Christian have money dealings with a Saracen except in such sort that he knows he cannot be cheated; for they strive to cheat us. . . .

§ Let the pilgrim beware of entering mosques, that is Saracen temples and oratories, because if found therein, he will in no case escape unharmed, even should he escape with his life. . . .

§ Pilgrims must not grudge to pay money to save themselves from the many annoyances which beset them, but when money has to be paid they must give it straightway without grumbling. . . .

§ The pilgrim must show respect to the poor convent of the brethren thereof, who dwell there among the infidels for the comfort of the pilgrims, and who are willing to serve pilgrims according to their means.

Brother Fabri's account of his journey well illustrates the situation which existed during the Mamluk and early Ottoman periods. European travelers could visit the main eastern Mediterranean cities without major difficulties, and there were arrangements for pilgrims to visit holy sites in Jerusalem as well as a few other places in the Holy Land. But otherwise the Middle East was practically non-accessible to the West.

This situation began to change toward the end of the 1700s. The Ottoman empire was in an advanced state of decline and found itself increasingly at the mercy of European powers and Russia. France and Britain, especially, recognized the political and commercial advantages of an increased presence in the Middle East. This was also an age of exploration for Europe, and a new breed of travelers began to push further and further into the interior of Egypt and the Fertile Crescent. Often they were obliged to travel in disguise to avoid suspicion and harassment. But they made careful observations and provided detailed accounts of what they saw. Among these eighteenth century adventurers were Richard Pococke and Karsten Niebuhr.

Richard Pococke, an Anglican clergyman, visited the Holy Land and ventured as far as Aswan in Upper (southern) Egypt in 1737. He visited and sketched the pyramids at Gizeh and Saqqara as well as the temple ruins at Philae, Karnak, Luxor, Denderah and Edfuh. His drawings were received in England with much enthusiasm. Scholars pondered the hieroglyphs which covered the Egyptian monuments, but it would be many years before these could be deciphered. There was considerable difference of opinion as to whether or not they actually represented a writing system.

Karsten Niebuhr, a Hanoverian in the service of Frederick V of Denmark, traveled throughout the Middle East with several other scholars from 1760 to 1767. All of his companions died during the trip, but he returned safely and wrote a fascinating book about his adventures. His descriptions are detailed and precise; he even made the first accurate transcriptions of cuneiform writing. These transcriptions could not be read, of course, because cuneiform writing had not yet been deciphered.

Napoleon invaded Egypt in 1798 with the intention of pushing through the Holy Land into Mesopotamia. From here he would be in a position to challenge the British hold on India. Napoleon was also interested in antiquities and scientific exploration. He had read Niebuhr's book and brought along a copy, and was accompanied by a large number of scholars representing various disciplines. The results of their investigations were published ten years later in a huge multivolume work entitled *Description de l'Egypte*. Two items are especially noteworthy: Napoleon's engineers prepared the first accurate map of Egypt and the Palestinian coast; the "Rosetta Stone" was discovered by his men at the village of Rosetta in the Nile delta. Later the Rosetta Stone would serve as the key for deciphering Egyptian hieroglyphic writing. Napoleon's campaign was less successful from a military point of view. He was halted at Acre in 1799, and his Mediterranean fleet was destroyed soon after by Admiral Nelson.

Claudius Rich. Following Napoleon's unsuccessful campaign, the British began a concerted effort to establish a presence of their own in the Middle East. In 1808 Britain successfully negotiated with the Ottoman government for permission to place a resident official for the British India Company in Baghdad. Claudius Rich was appointed to the post, which he used as a base for exploring the ancient ruins of Mesopotamia. He visited such sites as Babylon and Nineveh, made some small-scale excavations, and found a number of inscriptions. Rich's efforts significantly increased European interest in the antiquities of Mesopotamia.

Ludwig Burckhardt. Although Swiss by birth, Ludwig Burckhardt was commissioned by a British society to explore the interior of Africa. He taught himself Arabic and traveled through Syria, the Holy Land, Arabia and Egypt from 1809 to 1812 disguised as a poor wandering sheik. In the process he rediscovered Petra, the amazing capital of the Nabatean kingdom, and Abu Simbel with its colossal statues of Rameses II. Burckhardt's disguise allowed him to visit even Mecca, the holy city of Islam. Burckhardt died of dysentery in Cairo without achieving his main goal: exploring the interior of Africa. His travel journal was published posthumously and makes for fascinating reading.

The "Treasury" at Petra as seen by David Roberts in 1838

David Roberts. By the 1830s more and more westerners were traveling in the Middle East. This was especially true in Egypt and the Holy Land under the administration of Mohammed Ali (appointed Pasha of Egypt in 1808 and ruled the Holy Land and most of Syria, 1831-1839). Among these westerners were David Roberts, a British artist, and Edward Robinson, an American seminary professor. Roberts traveled throughout Egypt, Sinai and the Holy Land in 1838, making sketches of all he saw. His drawings have become increasingly valuable in recent years, not only because of their artistic value but because they provide glimpses of the people and monuments of the Middle East before photography.

Edward Robinson, a professor of Bible at Union Theological Seminary in New York, became concerned that so little was known about the geography and antiquities of the Holy Land during biblical times. In order to correct this situation, he made two extended trips there in 1838 and 1852. Robinson was well prepared for this undertaking, having thoroughly studied all the sources available in his day relevant to the geography and antiquities of the area. He had the help of a former student, Eli Smith, who had become a missionary to the Middle East and knew Arabic. Robinson and Smith traveled throughout the Holy Land on horseback, carefully observing the topographical features and Arabic place names, and comparing these with the biblical narratives and place names. As a result they were able to establish the locations of many biblical sites, including biblical Bethel. (See the discussion of "Ancient Names-Modern Names," below.)

Robinson published the results of their research in a three-volume work entitled *Biblical Researches in Palestine and Adjacent Regions*. This caught the attention of biblical scholars in the West and remains a very useful work. One of Robinson's contemporaries wrote: "The works of Robinson and Smith surpass the total of all previous contributions to Palestinian geography from the time of Eusebius and Jerome to the early nineteenth century."

Edward Robinson

Edward Robinson Rediscovers Ancient Bethel

The old city of Bethel plays an important role in the Old Testament. It was there that Jeroboam I set up one of the golden calves, for example, and that Amos preached (see scripture passages listed with Map 7 below). But the actual location of ancient Bethel was forgotten through the ages. Credit for its rediscovery goes to Edward Robinson. Exploring the vicinity north of Jerusalem on horseback in 1838, he realized that the little Arab village of Beitin must mark the ancient spot. In Robinson's own words,

> There is little room for question, that both the name and site of Beitin are identical with those of ancient Bethel. The latter was a border city between Benjamin and Ephraim; at first assigned to Benjamin, but conquered and afterwards retained by Ephraim. According to Eusebius and Jerome, it lay twelve Roman miles from Jerusalem, on the right or east of the road leading to Sichem or Neapolis (Nabulus). From Beitin to el-Bireh we found the distance to be forty-five minutes, and from Bireh to Jerusalem three hours, with horses. The correspondence therefore in the situation is very exact; and the name affords decisive confirmation. The Arabic termination *in* for the Hebrew *el*, is not an unusual change; we found indeed several other instances of it entirely parallel.

Deciphering Ancient Languages. By the 1850s, when Edward Robinson made his second visit to the Holy Land, scholars were making significant headway in deciphering the hieroglyphic writing of ancient Egypt and the cuneiform writing of ancient Mesopotamia.

• *Hieroglyphic texts from Egypt.* The ancient Egyptians developed a method of writing utilizing picture symbols. Eventually the ability to read this form of writing was lost. Travelers who saw the picture symbols carved on the ancient temples and elsewhere speculated that they had some sort of magical or mystical interpretation. Thus they called them "hieroglyphics," which means "holy pictures" in Greek. It was not until the end of the 1700s that scholars began to realize that hieroglyphics represented a systematic method of writing and began a concerted effort to decipher them. The Rosetta Stone, discovered by Napoleon's soldiers, proved to be the key.

Name and title of Rameses II in hieroglyphs

Inscribed on the Rosetta Stone are three versions of a royal decree from the reign of Ptolemy V (203-181 B.C.). One version is hieroglyphic, another demotic (cursive script developed from hieroglyphics ca. 600 B.C.), and still another is Greek. Scholars translated the Greek version of the decree with little difficulty, and through comparison were eventually able to decipher the hieroglyphic and demotic versions. Jean Francois Champollion, a young schoolteacher from Grenoble, made the first significant breakthrough. His famous *Lettre à M. Dacier*, outlining the basics of hieroglyphics, was delivered to the Paris Academy on September 29, 1822. This was only the beginning. It remained for Champollion and others to explore the details of Egyptian grammar, syntax and vocabulary. Also the thousands of hieroglyphic texts had to be copied from the temples, tombs and monuments in Egypt and then translated. At the beginning of the nineteenth century very little was known of ancient Egypt except for the scant information provided by the Old Testament and a few classical sources such as Herodotus. By the end of the nineteenth century it was possible to write massive volumes on ancient Egypt based upon first-hand Egyptian sources.

Fortunately, some of the new information derived from the hieroglyphic texts pertained specifically to the geography and history of the Holy Land. For example, the Egyptian pharaohs often undertook military campaigns in that direction and had accounts of their glory inscribed on public monuments for all to see. One of these monumental inscriptions from the reign of Pharaoh Merneptah (ca. 1230 B.C.) consists of a long hymn of praise to the gods whom Merneptah considered responsible for certain Egyptian victories in North Africa. Near the end of the hymn, mention is made of yet other Egyptian victories in the Holy Land. As indicated above, this is the earliest known reference to Israel in any written document outside of the Bible.

> The princes are prostrate, begging for peace
> Not one raises his head among the Nine Bows.
>> Tehenu is desolate;
>> Hatti is pacified;
>> Canaan is plundered with every evil;
>> Ashkelon is exiled;
>> Gezer has been seized;

Yanoam no longer exists;
Israel is laid waste, his seed is not;
Hurru is become a widow for Egypt!
All the lands together they are pacified; Everyone who was restless, he has been bound by the King of Upper and Lower Egypt: Ba-en-Re Meri-Amon; The Son of Re: Mer-ne-Ptah Hotep-hir-Maat, given life like Re every day.

• *Cuneiform texts from Mesopotamia.* The people of ancient Mesopotamia also developed a form of writing utilizing picture symbols. But they generally wrote on clay tablets with a stylus (triangular tipped reed) so that the picture symbols soon became "stylized" to the extent that they look like a sequence of configurations of wedges. Scholars call this form of writing "cuneiform" from the Latin *cuneus* ("wedge"). Cuneiform script was used to write several different languages, including Sumerian, Babylonian, Hittite, Ugaritic and Old Persian.

Cuneiform script used in this instance to write the Ugaritic alphabet

Niebuhr brought back some fairly accurate transcriptions of cuneiform writings from Persepolis. Later travelers provided European scholars with more examples, and in 1802 a German school master, Georg Friedrich Grotefend, made a significant breakthrough toward their decipherment. A convincing translation of a long cuneiform text was not possible for another four decades, however, until Henry C. Rawlinson retrieved a good copy of the Behistun Inscription.

Rawlinson was a British army officer who had spent his childhood in India where he learned Persian. The Behistun Inscription is a part of a huge bas-relief carved in a rocky cliff overlooking the route of an ancient highway which connected Babylon and Persia. The inscription, which is some 350 feet above the base of the cliff, recounts the exploits of Darius the Great in three languages: ancient Persian, Median and Babylonian. After managing to make a plaster overlay copy of the text, and relying on his knowledge of modern Persian, Rawlinson published a translation of the ancient Persian column in 1846. Later he was able to work out the Median column, and finally, in 1851, he published a translation of one hundred and twelve lines of the Babylonian column.

Letter from Abdu-Heba of Jerusalem

The Amarna Letters, discovered in the el-Amarna district of Egypt during the 1880s, are particularly illuminating in regard to Syro-Palestinian politics prior to the Israelite settlement. These late Bronze Age Letters, written in cuneiform on clay tablets, are correspondences between Asiatic vassals and their Egyptian overlord. The following letter was from Abdu-Heba, Egyptian-appointed governor of Jerusalem during the mid-fifteenth century B.C.

To my lord the king say: Thus Abdu-Heba, thy servant.

Seven times and again seven times I fall before the feet of my lord the king. What have I done to my lord the king? They accuse me before my lord the king, saying: "Abdu-Heba has rebelled against his lord the king." But it was neither my father nor my mother who placed me in this office; it was the arm of the mighty king who allowed me to succeed my father. So why should I commit transgression against my lord the king?

As long as my lord the king lives, I will challenge the king's commissioner, saying: "Why do you favor the Apiru and oppose the governors?" It is on this basis that I am accused in the presence of my lord the king. It is being said that the lands of my lord the king are lost and that I am at fault. But the king should know that Yanhamu reassigned the garrison which the king sent here...O king, my lord, there are no garrison troops here. Let the king take care of his land! The king is urged to take care of his land! The king's lands have all rebelled, and Ilimilku is the one who is stirring up the rebellion. So let the king take care of his land! I want to come and explain the situation eye-to-eye, but the hostility against me is so strong that I dare not enter into the presence of my lord the king. So may it please the king to send me a garrison of troops in order that I may come safely and see the two eyes of my lord the king.

As truly as my lord the king lives, when the commissioner makes his round I will have to report that the king's lands are lost. Do you not hear what I am saying? All of the governors are lost; my lord the king does not have a single governor left. The king is urged to send archers. Let my lord the king send troops of archers or the king will have no lands left. The Apiru plunder all of the king's territories. If archers are sent this year the lands of my lord the king can be saved; but if they are not sent the lands will be lost.

To the scribe of my lord the king: Thus Abdu-Heba, thy servant. Present eloquent words to my lord the king. All the lands of my lord the king are lost!

This extraordinary discovery altered the understanding of the history and literature of the peoples of Mesopotamia in the same way that Champollion's decipherment of hieroglyphics revolutionized our knowledge of ancient Egypt. Other languages written in cuneiform script have since been deciphered (Sumerian, Hittite, Ugaritic), and entire libraries and royal archives have been discovered. The royal archive discovered at Tell Mardikh (the ancient city-state of Ebla) in 1974 is the most recent instance. Ebla flourished during the Early Bronze Age; its inhabitants spoke a proto-Canaanite dialect, but they wrote their language on clay in cuneiform script.

As with the hieroglyphic texts from Egypt, the cuneiform documents provided new information concerning the geography and history of the Holy Land. For example, the Assyrian kings Shalmaneser III (858-824 B.C.), Adad-nirari III (810-783 B.C.), Tiglath-pilser III (744-727 B.C.), Sargon II (721-705 B.C.) and Sennacherib (704-681 B.C.) all made reference in their royal annals to Israelite kings or cities.

• *Canaanite Inscriptions.* The peoples of Syria, Phoenicia and the Holy Land spoke various closely related dialects; for lack of a better term, scholars generally refer to these related dialects as "Canaanite." Among these were Ugaritic, Phoenician, Hebrew, Moabite and Edomite. Our earliest known example (Ugaritic) is written in cuneiform. Later examples (Phoenician, Hebrew, Moabite) are written in an alphabetic script probably developed near the end of the Bronze Age. This is sometimes called the "Phoenician Alphabet," not necessarily because the Phoenicians invented it, but because they transmitted it to the Greeks and Romans, and ultimately, to the whole western world.

The Mesha Inscription

No extensive archives written in this old Canaanite (Phoenician) alphabetic script have been discovered. Some very interesting inscriptions have turned up however—the Mesha Inscription, for example, discovered at the site of ancient Dibon, southern Transjordan, in 1868. The following are the opening five lines of the Mesha Inscription in the original Canaanite script and in translation (see pages 66-67 for a translation of the full inscription).

I am Mesha, Son of Chemoshyatti,
king of Moab, the Dibonite.
My father reigned over Moab thirty years and I reigned after my father.
And I built this sanctuary to Chemosh at Qahoh. . .because he saved me from all
the kings and caused me to triumph over my adversaries.
Omri, king of Israel, oppressed Moab for a long time because Chemosh was
    angry with us.
His son succeeded him and said, "I too will oppress Moab!"

The Aramaeans developed a squared form of this old Canaanite (Phoenician) script which gradually replaced the latter during the Persian period. The following are the same five lines of the Mesha Inscription transcribed into the squared Aramaic script.

אנך·משע·בן·כמש .. מלך·מאב·הד
יבני | אבי·מלך·על·מאב·שלשן·שת·ואנך·מלך
תי·אחר·אבי | ואעש·הבמת·זאת·לכמש·בקרהה | בנ.ס.[י]
שע·כי·השעני·מכל·ה . לכן·וכי·הראני·בכל·שנאי | עמר
י·מלך·ישראל·ויענו·את·מאב·ימן·רבן·כי·יאנף·כמש·באר

The books of the Old Testament, originally written in the Canaanite script, were later recopied and handed down in the squared Aramaic script.

Archaeology. Gradually, as scholars learned more about ancient times and began to search for the remains of past civilizations more methodically, a new discipline emerged: archaeology. Much of the information presented in this guidebook has become available through archaeological research.

The term "archaeology" is at times used rather loosely. Perhaps it will be beneficial to introduce a working definition.

Archaeology: The *search for* and *study of artifactual remains* from *past civilizations.*

• *"The search for . . ."* Archaeologists explore the sites where people lived during the past, probe into the ruins and debris which remain, and collect and systematically record anything which might provide clues as to who these people were and what their lifestyle was like.

Archaeological excavations underway at et-Tell (biblical Ai)

• *". . . and study of . . ."* Archaeologists do not excavate "facts" at the ancient sites. They uncover objects—broken pieces of pottery, foundations of walls, collapsed roofs, discarded weapons, tools and other objects. These finds must be interpreted, involving what is already known from written records and / or from excavations at other related sites. Actually, archaeologists usually spend many more hours in libraries than they do in the field.

- *". . . artifactual remains . . ."* Generally, a distinction is made between the historian, who attempts to reconstruct the past on the basis of written documents, and the archaeologist, who deals with artifacts, non-written remains. But in the Middle East this distinction tends to break down because so many of the written documents have been recovered by archaeologists in the process of their excavations.

- *". . . past civilizations."* Archaeologists are concerned with the material traces of human activity, products of past civilizations. Thus archaeology is to be distinguished from geology which has to do with the earth itself, and paleontology, which has to do with the physical structure of early life forms (fossils and bones).

The Holy Land
during Biblical Times

Ancient Names—Modern Names. "Holy Land" is a rather vague geographical designation for the southern part of the eastern Mediterranean seaboard, the southwestern end of the Fertile Crescent. More specifically, the Holy Land may be identified as the area immediately south of the Lebanon and Anti-Lebanon mountain ranges, bounded to the west by the Mediterranean Sea, to the east by the Arabian Desert, and to the south by the Sinai Peninsula. The west-east distance from the Mediterranean Sea to the desert fringe averages about 60 to 70 miles. The north-south distance, from the foot of the Lebanon Mountains to the Negeb (the arid northeastern fringe of the Sinai Peninsula) is hardly more than 150 miles.

Thus the total area of the Holy Land approximates that of the state of Vermont or the country of Belgium. At the same time, it must be emphasized that there is considerable variance within this small area with regard to terrain, climate, and agricultural possibilities. Sandwiched between sea and desert, surely the most dramatic topographical feature of the Holy Land is the Jordan Valley with its Sea of Galilee, Jordan River, and Dead Sea.

From earliest times the Holy Land has been identified by a variety of names, often with a distinction made between the area west of the Jordan River and the area to the east. In the Old Testament, for example, the area west of the Jordan is usually called "Canaan" and the area to the east simply "beyond the Jordan." "Palestine" is the English pronunciation of "Philistia" (land of the Philistines) which in Old Testament usage pertains to the narrow strip of coastal plain south of approximately where Tel Aviv stands today. Greek and Roman geographers began to use the name Philistia in a broader sense, inclusive of the whole area between the Mediterranean Sea and the desert fringe. During the Mandate period Palestine was the official designation of the area between the Sea and the Jordan River. Today the Holy Land falls within the boundaries of the Hashemite Kingdom of Jordan, the state of Israel, and certain territories under Israeli military control.

Just as the Holy Land itself has been called by different names during the past, so too have its mountains, valleys and cities. Keeping all the names and name changes straight is much easier once it is realized that they tend to correspond to four major phases of history, as outlined below.

(1) *From earliest times to the conquest of Alexander the Great.* The earliest inhabitants of the Holy Land, at least as far back as we have written records, were Semitic speaking peoples (Canaanites, Moabites, Israelites, among others). Naturally, they used names based on their Semitic languages.

(2) *The Hellenistic-Roman-Byzantine Periods.* Beginning with Alexander the Great's conquest in the fourth century B.C., the Holy Land was dominated by Greek- and Latin-speaking people for a thousand years. These new-comers relpaced many of the old semitic names with new ones derived from Greek and Latin. When, in certain cases, Semitic names were retained, they usually were pronounced in a fashion more compatible with Greek and Latin.

(3) *From the Arab Expansion to the Present.* Arabic is a Semitic language similar to Canaanite, Moabite and Hebrew. Thus, when the Arabs occupied the Holy Land during the seventh century A.D., many of the old Semitic names reemerged. Under Arabic influence, of course, they were pro-nounced differently. The Arabs also introduced new names of their own derivation.

(4) *Modern Israeli Names.* There has been a tendency on the part of the Israelis to name their new settlements after biblical cities while replacing Arab names with Hebrew equivalents. The Israeli settlements named after biblical cities often are not situated on the actual biblical sites, however. Modern Arad, for example, is several miles from the site of ancient Arad.

Biblical Cities Whose Names Have Changed

Rabbah was the main city of the Ammonites in Old Testament times. It was rebuilt by Ptolemy II during the Hellenistic period and renamed *Philadelphia*. Later, during the Arabic period, it reemerged as *Amman*, preserving the memory of ancient Ammonites. Today it is the capital city of Jordan.

Jerusalem was destroyed and rebuilt by Hadrian in the second century A.D. The new name he selected for the city was *Aelia*

Capitolina. Later, during the Arabic period, it came to be called *el-Quds* ("the holy place"). Today, under the Israeli government, its official name is again *Jerusalem*.

Beth Shean, the city where the bodies of Saul and Jonathan were taken after their deaths on Mt. Gilboa (1 Samuel 31:10), was renamed *Scythopolis* during the Roman period. During the Arab period the old name would reemerge as *Beisan*. Today on Israeli maps it appears as *Bet She'an*.

Hebron, known in the Old Testament as the burial place of Abraham and Sarah, kept the same name during the Hellenistic and Roman periods. The traditional Arabic name, however, is *el-Khalil* ("the friend"); Abraham is known in the Koran as the "friend of Allah." It appears again as *Hebron* on Israeli maps.

Acco, according to Judges 1:31-32, remained in Canaanite hands long after the Israelites settled Canaan. It was already an old city, mentioned in earlier Egyptian documents as *'Aka*. The Assyrians, who conquered the city in 733 B.C., called it *Akku*. During the Hellenistic period it was renamed *Ptolemais*, probably due to its refortification by Ptolemy II. It is called Ptolemais in Acts 21:7. The Crusaders, who held the city for almost 200 years, called it *St. Jean d'Acre*. Today it is called simply *Acre*.

Old Testament Times. The Old Testament books date from the earliest of the four historical phases outlined above, during which the ancient Semitic names were still in use. Maps 4-7 represent the land as it was known at that time and indicate geographical terms and place names which appear in the Old Testament. These Old Testament terms and names are italicized in the explanations below; see also the glossary of geographical terms in the reference section below.

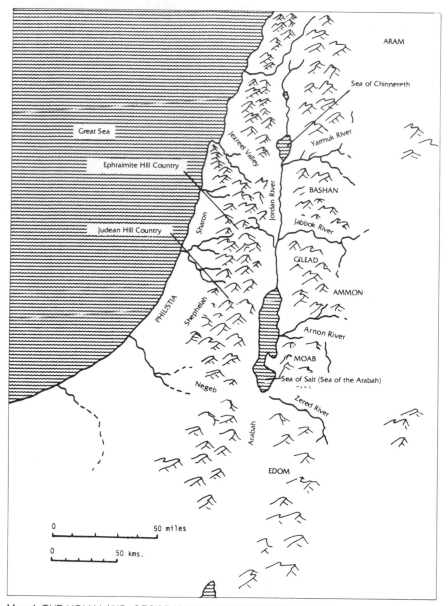

Map 4: THE HOLY LAND: GEOGRAPHICAL TERMS FROM OLD TESTAMENT TIMES

Map 4: Geographical Features. The *Sea of Chinnereth* (later called the Sea of Galilee or Lake of Tiberias), the *Jordan River*, and the *Sea of Salt* (also called *Sea of Arabah* in the Old Testament and later the Dead Sea) all lie within a deep depression termed the *Arabah* by the ancient Israelites and the "Ghor" by Arabs. In fact the Arabah/Ghor is part of a massive geological rift beginning in Syria and extending through east Africa to Mozambique. The Red Sea is also formed by this rift.

Paralleling the Arabah/Ghor on the east, between it and the desert, is a strip of rugged but adequately watered and cultivable ground which Old Testament writers either referred to as *beyond the Jordan* or called by various regional names: *Bashan, Gilead, Ammon, Moab* and *Edom.* Four rivers flow into the Arabah/Ghor from the east. Three of these are mentioned in the Old Testament: The *Jabbok*, today called the Nahr ez-Zerqa; the *Arnon*, or Wady Mujib; and the *Zered*, modern Wady Hesa. The fourth river, not mentioned in the Old Testament, is the Yarmuk.

West of the Arabah and also paralleling it is a spine of mountains broken at one point by the *Jezreel Valley*. The Old Testament writers usually referred to the various parts of these mountains by the names of the local tribes—for example, *Ephraimite hill country* and *Judean hill country*. Between the mountains and the Sea is the coastal plain, where a distinction was made between *Philistia*, the southern part of the coastal plain, and *Sharon*, further to the north where the plain is more narrow. The intermediate foothills between the Judean hill country and Philistia were known as the *Shephelah*. South of the Judean hill country on the fringe of the Sinai desert was the *Negeb*.

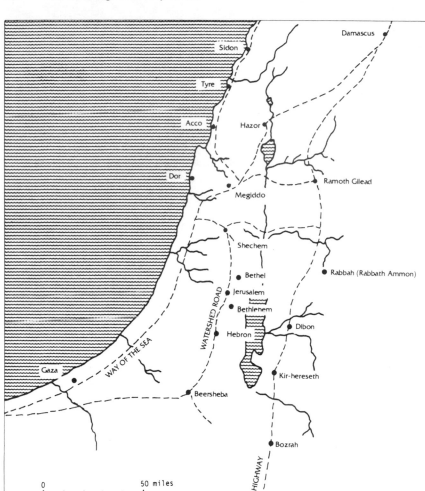

Map 5: MAIN ROADS AND CITIES DURING OLD TESTAMENT TIMES

Map 5: Main Roads and Cities during Old Testament Times. Two major trade routes passed through the Holy Land in ancient times; assuredly, they would be major international highways today if the political situation allowed. One of these is known as the *Way of the Sea* in the Old Testament (Isaiah 9:1) and the Via Maris in later classical sources. It began in the Egyptian delta, continued through the coastal plain, eventually crossed a northwestern spur of the central hill country, and entered the Jezreel Valley. The route then branched, one branch continuing northwest toward the Phoenician coast, another northeast toward Damascus, and yet another eastward across the Jordan.

The second major trade route led northward from Arabia and the Red Sea, served the Transjordan, and continued to Damascus. This may be what Numbers 20:17 and 21:22 refer to as the *King's Highway*. The Romans paved this route in the second century A.D. and added heavy stone distance markers ("milestones"). Their name for it was the Via Nova ("New Road").

A third route of less international importance proceeded north-south along the watershed of the mountains west of the Jordan. Also several east-west roads crossed these mountains at places where valleys made crossing easier.

It will be obvious from Map 5 that many of the cities and villages mentioned in the Old Testament were situated along the main thoroughfares. *Bozrah* (capital city of the Edomites), *Kir-hereseth* and *Dibon* (chief cities of the Moabites) and *Rabbah* (capital of the Ammonites) were on or

near the King's Highway. *Hebron, Bethlehem, Jerusalem, Bethel* and *Shechem* were all on the north-south watershed road. Some of the cities were especially important due to their strategic locations. *Megiddo* (spelled "Armageddon" in Greek, see Revelation 16:16) was the scene of many battles in ancient times because it controlled the pass through which the Way of the Sea progressed, connecting the coastal plain with the Jezreel Valley.

Roman milestone along the Via Nova

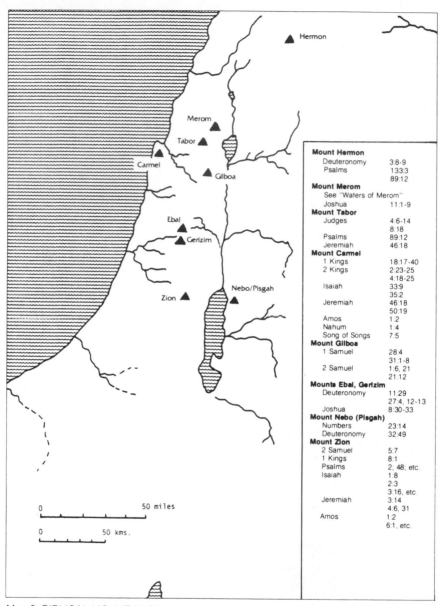

The following reference list appears within the map:

Mount Hermon
Deuteronomy	3:8-9
Psalms	133:3
	89:12

Mount Merom
See "Waters of Merom"	
Joshua	11:1-9

Mount Tabor
Judges	4:6-14
	8:18
Psalms	89:12
Jeremiah	46:18

Mount Carmel
1 Kings	18:17-40
2 Kings	2:23-25
	4:18-25
Isaiah	33:9
	35:2
Jeremiah	46:18
	50:19
Amos	1:2
Nahum	1:4
Song of Songs	7:5

Mount Gilboa
1 Samuel	28:4
	31:1-8
2 Samuel	1:6, 21
	21:12

Mounts Ebal, Gerizim
Deuteronomy	11:29
	27:4, 12-13
Joshua	8:30-33

Mount Nebo (Pisgah)
Numbers	23:14
Deuteronomy	32:49

Mount Zion
2 Samuel	5:7
1 Kings	8:1
Psalms	2; 48; etc.
Isaiah	1:8
	2:3
	3:16, etc.
Jeremiah	3:14
	4:6, 31
Amos	1:2
	6:1, etc.

Map labels: Hermon, Merom, Tabor, Carmel, Gilboa, Ebal, Gerizim, Zion, Nebo/Pisgah

0 ———— 50 miles

0 ———— 50 kms.

Map 6: BIBLICAL MOUNTAINS

Map 6: Nine Biblical Mountains. Nine mountain tops are conspicuous in the Holy Land and receive special mention in the Old Testament. *Mount Hermon*, a spur of the Anti-Lebanon range, towers in the north. *Mount Tabor* is prominent in the Jezreel Valley. Joshua defeated a coalition of northern kings who had "encamped together at the *waters of Merom*." The waters of Merom probably are to be associated with Mount Merom overlooking the Sea of Galilee, although the mountain itself is not actually mentioned in the Old Testament.

Mount Carmel, jutting out into the Mediterranean Sea, perhaps is best known from the story of Elijah's contest with the prophets of Baal. But Carmel is mentioned in a number of other Old Testament contexts as well. Jeremiah, for example, anticipating the destruction of Egypt, prophesies:

> As I live, says the King, whose name is the lord of hosts,
>   like *Tabor* among the mountains, and like *Carmel* by the sea,
>   shall one come.

> Prepare yourselves baggage for exile, O inhabitants of Egypt!
>   For Memphis shall become a waste, a ruin,
>   without habitation.

Saul and Jonathan were killed in battle on *Mount Gilboa* and their bodies taken to the city of Beth Shean by the Philistines. The twin mountains, *Ebal* and *Gerizim*, overlook a pass guarded by the famous city of Shechem. It was here that Joshua assembled the Israelites and uttered a stirring challenge: "Choose this day whom ye shall serve . . . but as for me and my house we will serve the LORD" (Joshua 24). Moses viewed the promised land from *Mount Nebo*, also called *Pisgah*.

Threshing
wheat
on
Mount
Nebo

Surely the most important mountain to the biblical writers was *Mount Zion*, the site of Solomon's temple.

> The LORD roars from *Zion*, and utters his voice from Jerusalem;
> The pastures of the shepherds mourn, and the top of Carmel withers.

Look up the passages cited in the margin of Map 6.

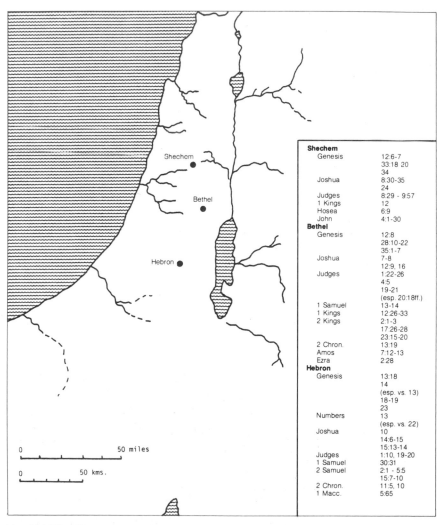

Shechem		
	Genesis	12:6-7
		33:18 20
		34
	Joshua	8:30-35
		24
	Judges	8:29 - 9:57
	1 Kings	12
	Hosea	6:9
	John	4:1-30
Bethel		
	Genesis	12:8
		28:10-22
		35:1-7
	Joshua	7-8
		12:9, 16
	Judges	1:22-26
		4:5
		19-21
		(esp. 20:18ff.)
	1 Samuel	13-14
	1 Kings	12:26-33
	2 Kings	2:1-3
		17:26-28
		23:15-20
	2 Chron.	13:19
	Amos	7:12-13
	Ezra	2:28
Hebron		
	Genesis	13:18
		14
		(esp. vs. 13)
		18-19
		23
	Numbers	13
		(esp. vs. 22)
	Joshua	10
		14:6-15
		15:13-14
	Judges	1:10, 19-20
	1 Samuel	30:31
	2 Samuel	2:1 - 5:5
		15:7-10
	2 Chron.	11:5, 10
	1 Macc.	5:65

0   50 miles

0   50 kms.

Map 7: SHECHEM, BETHEL, HEBRON

Map 7: Shechem, Bethel, Hebron. Genesis 12-13 recounts Abraham's initial entry into the Land of Canaan and his north-south passage through it. We are told that he encamped and constructed altars at three points, all reported in rather specific detail. He camped and built an altar first *at the oak of Moreh, near Shechem*, next *on the mountain between Bethel and Ai*, and finally *at the oaks of Mamre, near Hebron.*

Modern readers unfamiliar with the land of the Bible tend to disregard such geographical details. The ancient Israelites knew very well where these places were; and stories became more dramatic and meaningful for them as a result. All three locations were important sanctuaries during Old Testament times, and the three cities involved—Shechem, Bethel, Hebron—played crucial roles throughout biblical history.

Watering goats
near Hebron

Shechem, as indicated above, guarded the pass between Mounts Ebal and Gerizim and was the setting of Joshua's famous farewell address. It was here that the northern tribes assembled after Solomon's death to decide whether they should remain loyal to "the house of David" or establish a separate kingdom of their own (they opted for the latter, with Jeroboam I their first king). Nearby, but much later, Jesus confronted the woman at Jacob's well.

Not only was *Bethel* the setting of Jacob's dream, it was here that Jeroboam I erected one of the golden calves. Amos preached at Bethel but was forced to leave after his critical remarks aimed at Jeroboam II.

Abraham purchased the cave of Machpelah near *Hebron* as a burial place for his family. The Hebronites crowned David king before he was recognized by the remainder of Israel; Hebron served as David's capital for seven and a half years. Later, after Jerusalem had replaced Hebron as David's capital, the Hebronites would support Absalom's bid for the throne.

Look up the passages listed in the margin of Map 7 for more details about these cities in biblical times.

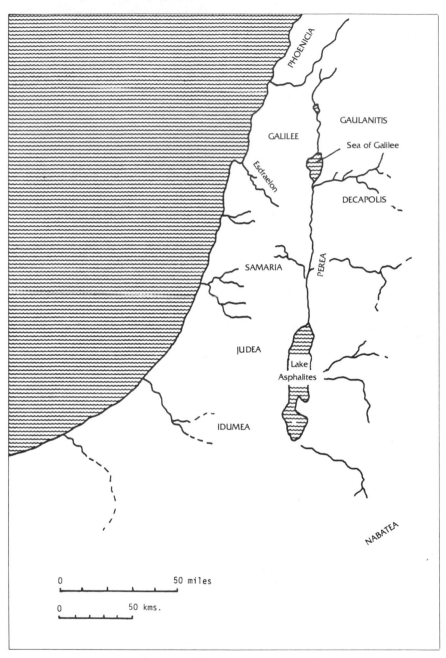

Map 8: GEOGRAPHICAL TERMS FROM NEW TESTAMENT TIMES

New Testament Times. While the Old Testament books date from the earliest of the four historical phases outlined above, during which time the ancient Semitic place names and geographical terms were still in use, the New Testament books date from the second historical phase when there was a tendency to replace the old Semitic names with new ones based on Greek and Latin. Often it was simply a matter of new pronunciations for the old names: Jezreel became *Esdraelon*; Heshbon was now pronounced *Esbus*; Megiddo became *Armageddon*. In other cases complete name changes occurred: Acco was renamed Ptolemais; Beth Shean became *Scythopolis*; Rabbah of the Ammonites became *Philadelphia*. When new settlements were founded they received totally new names, such as *Neapolis*, *Gadara*, and *Tiberias*.

By New Testament times the mountainous area north of Jezreel/Esdraelon had come to be called *Galilee*. Correspondingly, the Sea of Chinnereth was known as the Sea of Galilee. The central mountains, extending from Jezreel/Esdraelon to the vicinity of Jerusalem, were called *Samaria*, while those further south, extending from the Jerusalem area to Hebron's environs, were called *Judea*. The highlands of northern Transjordan often were referred to collectively as the *Decapolis* because of a political league of approximately ten cities clustered in that area. Decapolis means "ten cities" in Greek. The territory directly east of the Jordan river, opposite Samaria, was called *Parea*. Perea means "beyond" in Greek.

Following the Babylonian devastation of the kingdom of Judah in the sixth century B.C., Edomites apparently entered the hill country and Negeb south of Hebron. This area still had a largely Edomite population in New Testament times and accordingly was called *Idumea* (Greek equivalent of "Edom"). Southern Transjordan on the other hand, which had been the core of Edomite territory in Old Testament times, was now dominated by the Nabateans and known as *Nabatea*. Historians are uncertain of the origin of the Nabateans.

The two major trade routes traversing the Holy Land during Old Testament times were especially active during the Roman period, but they too were called by different names. What had been the Way of the Sea in Old Testament times was now called the *Via Maris*. It connected the Roman Empire with Egypt and North Africa. The old route through the Transjordan to Arabia, possibly the King's Highway mentioned in Numbers 20 and 21, was paved and fortified by Trajan and called the *Via Nova* ("New Road").

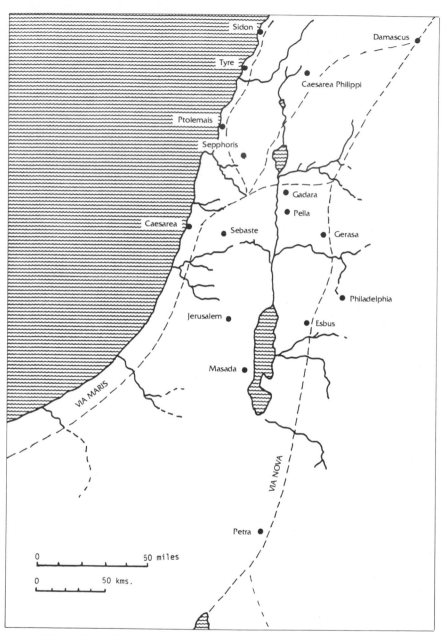

Map 9: MAIN ROADS AND CITIES DURING NEW TESTAMENT TIMES

Map 9 indicates the main roads and cities of the Holy Land during New Testament times. Except for Jerusalem, Jesus' ministry occurred primarily in and around the smaller villages of the land, especially in southern Galilee (Nazareth, Cana, Naim) and along the shore of the Sea of Galilee (Capernaum, Beth-saida).

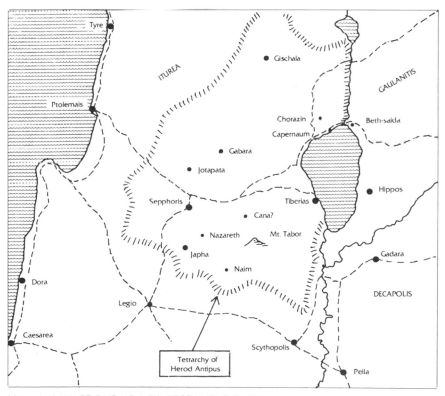

Map 10: GALILEE DURING NEW TESTAMENT TIMES

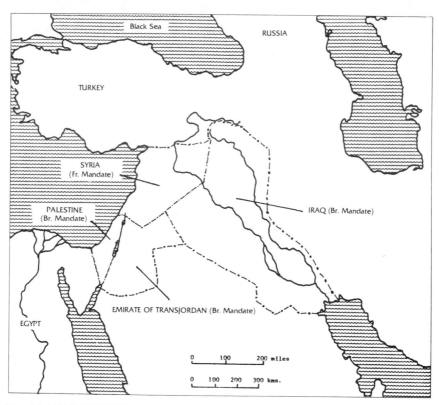

Map 11: MANDATE TERRITORIES FOLLOWING WORLD WAR I

Arabs and Israelis

World War I and Aftermath. Not only is the Holy Land the land of the Bible, it is today the scene of a bitter conflict between Arabs and Israelis. In essence, this is a conflict between two groups of disenfranchised peoples struggling for national autonomy: Jewish refugees from Russia, central Europe and other parts of the Middle East who have succeeded in establishing a modern Jewish nation including within its boundaries a large segment of the Holy Land; the indigenous Arab population of this segment of land who have been faced with the option of remaining under a Jewish government or fleeing what has been for many of them their own homeland for hundreds of years.

In terms of international diplomacy, the roots of the conflict go back to World War I. Diplomatic exchanges made during the war had the effect of conflicting promises to three different peoples. The Arabs were led to believe that Syria (understood in a broad geographical sense which would include Lebanon and the Holy Land) would become independent Arab territory (McMahon-Hussein letters, 1915; Anglo-French Declaration, 1918). The Jews were promised a national homeland in Palestine (Balfour Declaration, 1917). And France was assured that her claim to much of the Syrian coast would be recognized (Sykes-Picot Agreement, 1916). As it turned out, the League of Nations adopted a mandate concept as the guiding principle for dealing with the emancipated territories in the Middle East, which satisfied neither the Arabs nor the Jews. The mandate divisions were worked out at the San Remo Peace Conference which began in April 1920 and were approved by the League of Nations in July 1922. Specifically:

- France received Syria (including the interior and what is now Lebanon).

- England received Mesopotamia, where they installed a monarchy under British protection. The first king was Faisal, son of Sharif Hussein of Mecca (see below).

- England also received the Holy Land, which was divided into two parts: The territory west of the Jordan was designated "Palestine" and administered directly by a British mandate government; the territory east of the Jordan was declared an emirate (Arabic for "kingdom") under British protection.

The Hashemite Kingdom of Jordan. Hussein Ibn Ali, Sharif of Mecca, and his four sons (Ali, Faisal, Abdullah and Zaid), led an Arab uprising against the Turks during World War I. They were urged to do so by the British, encouraged by the famous "Lawrence of Arabia," and promised independence at the end of the war. Naturally the Arabs were disappointed by the League of Nations' decision to treat the Middle East as mandate territories. The details of the San Remo agreement were worked out by July of 1920, and in October of that same year Abdullah marched northward into the Transjordan toward Damascus with a Bedouin army. It was in this context that the British decided to establish the Emirate of the Transjordan under British protection and with Abdullah as emir (king). As his capital, Abdullah chose Amman, at this time little more than a village.

Britain granted limited independence to the Emirate of the Transjordan in 1923 but remained suzerain while reserving the right to maintain military bases there. At the end of World War II, prompted by the loyalty of Abdullah's government, Britain recognized the kingdom as fully independent. May 25, 1946, is celebrated as Independence Day.

Abdullah and his young kingdom joined the Arab attack on Israel following the U.N. resolution for partition and Israel's proclamation of independence in 1948. When the initial fighting ended, Israel had successfully defended borders which included a large part of the former mandate of Palestine, but Abdullah's troops occupied the central hill country, or the "West Bank" (see below). In 1950 the people of the West Bank, including the old city (Arab sector) of Jerusalem, decided by referendum to join the Emirate of Transjordan, now to be called simply Jordan. The following year, while worshiping at the al-Aksa Mosque in Jerusalem, Abdullah was assassinated. Jordan lost control of the West Bank as a result of the so-called Six Day War in 1967.

Abdullah was succeeded by his son, Talal. It soon became apparent that Talal would be unable to rule because of illness, and Talal's son, Hussein, was proclaimed king on August 11, 1952. Hussein was seventeen years old at the time.

The kingdom is known today as the Hashemite Kingdom of Jordan.

"Hashemite" refers to the family line, through which the royal family traces its ancestry back to Mohammed.

The State of Israel. The unsuccessful Jewish revolts against the Romans during the first and second centuries A.D., followed by the rapid Christianization of the Middle East during the third and fourth centuries, resulted in a sharp decline of Jewish presence in the Holy Land. Jewish communities continued to exist, but the Holy Land remained essentially non-Jewish until modern times. In the present century this situation has been changed radically as a result of Jewish immigration.

Although there was some Jewish immigration to the Holy Land during the late 1800s, largely due to Russian pogroms, Jewish immigration began to increase sharply after World War I. The Balfour Declaration in 1917 implied Britain's intention to create a Jewish state in Palestine; and by the late 1930s Hitler had come to power and begun his attacks on Jews in central Europe. Consider the following statistics:

At the beginning of World War I Palestine's population was 90% Arab, with the Jewish community numbering approximately 85,000.

During the three years alone after Hitler's appointment as chancellor, 1933-36, the Jewish population jumped from 230,000 to 400,000.

By 1947 the Jewish community had reached 650,000 or approximately one-third of the total population.

Initially there was no serious tension between the Arabs and the Jews. By the mid-1930s, however, the shift in population ratio was becoming obvious and the Jews were becoming more insistent in their demands for a partitioned Jewish state. There were constant acts of violence perpetrated by both Arabs and Jews in the 1930s and 1940s, while the British attempted unsuccessfully to curb Jewish immigration. Although various plans were offered for the partition of a Jewish state, none were acceptable to all parties concerned, and the matter remained unresolved until the end of World War II.

On November 29, 1947, the United Nations passed a resolution favoring the establishment of a Jewish state in Palestine. The British announced that they would terminate their mandate on May 14, 1948, and withdraw. Upon the British withdrawal, Israel proclaimed itself an independent nation and a full-scale Arab-Israeli war broke out. The young nation was able to defend its sovereignty and armistice agreements were signed in 1949. Full-scale warfare again exploded in 1956 (the Port Said Incident), 1967 (the "Six Day War") and 1973 (the "Yom Kippur War").

Israel's parliament, the Knesset, holds legislative power. The Knesset elects the president, who serves for a five-year term as nominal head of state and appoints the prime minister. The prime minister holds the executive power and remains in office as long as he/she has majority support from the Knesset.

Israel's Prime Ministers	
Ben-Gurion	1948-1953
Sharett	1953-1955
Ben Gurion	1955-1963
Eshkol	1963-1969
Golda Meir	1969-1974
Rabin	1974-1977
Begin	1977-

Present-Day Boundaries. Israel's borders remained essentially the same from the armistice in 1949 until 1967. As a result of the 1967 war, Israel gained military control of territories previously governed by surrounding Arab states and which today still have predominantly Arab populations. Map 12 indicates Israel's borders before and after the 1967 war. Note that Sinai (excluding the Gaza Strip) has been returned to Egypt as a result of the Camp David Accord. The following are explanations of some key terms:

• **Palestinian**. The term Palestinian, as used in the public media today, refers to Arabs whose ancestral homes are situated within the territory controlled now by Israel. Many of these people have fled to other countries, including Jordan, Syria, Lebanon, Brazil and the United States. Others remain with their homes and now are subject to the Israeli government. Those who fled wish to maintain their identity as a distinct people, and those who remained generally do not hold Israeli citizenship or have normal access to Israeli courts. Certainly then, they do not think of themselves as Israelis—they prefer to be called Palestinians.

• **Golan Heights**. Following the armistice between Israel and the Arab nations in 1949, the upper Jordan Valley immediately north of the Sea of Galilee remained in dispute. The Arabs insisted that the armistice agreements designated this valley as "no-man's land"; Israel contended that it belonged to her and established farm settlements on it. Thereupon Syria, which commanded the heights overlooking the valley on the east, began to shell the Israeli settlers below. These heights, known as the Golan Heights, were a source of anguish for the Israelis, who conquered them during the 1967 war at great expense in human life.

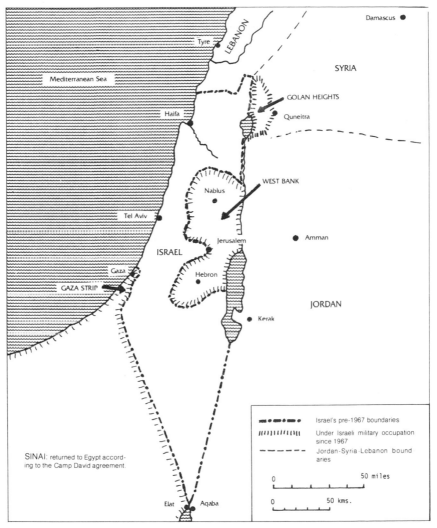

MAP 12: PRESENT-DAY BOUNDARIES OF THE HOLY LAND

• **West Bank**. The original boundaries of the state of Israel excluded a large section of territory immediately west of the Jordan River and the Dead Sea. This hill country was governed by the Hashemite Kingdom of Jordan from 1950 to 1967, and its population is almost entirely Arab. Many of the Palestinian refugees who fled Israel during 1947 and 1948 settled in refugee camps in this area. As a result of the 1967 war, this territory fell into Israeli hands, and it remains under Israeli military control. Israel insists that her continued control of this area is necessary for national defense and refers to it officially by the old biblical names—Judea and Samaria. The Arabs insist, and much of the international community tends to agree, that any reasonable peace settlement must involve a return of this territory to Arab hands. Those who hold the latter position prefer the name "West Bank" for this disputed territory.

• **Gaza Strip**. The Gaza Strip represents a similar situation. The city of Gaza, a narrow strip of territory which connects it with Sinai, and Sinai itself, were governed by Egypt prior to 1967. Gaza and the Gaza Strip have an especially dense Arab population because many Palestinians fled there when Israel was established in 1948. But this territory likewise was taken by Israel in 1967, and Israel holds it today. Sinai also fell to Israel in 1967 but was returned to Egypt as a result of the Camp David Accord.

_____ Part Two

Exploring the Land

Some General
Considerations

It would take many years to explore all of the interesting sites in the Holy Land. Part II will focus on the highlights, the places which deserve a visit even by those with only limited time to explore. These places of special interest will be treated in accordance with five suggested itineraries:

1. The King's Highway to Petra
2. Gilead, Bashan and the Decapolis
3. Jerusalem and Vicinity
4. The Southern Hill Country, Negeb and Dead Sea Valley
5. The Northern Hill Country, Mediterranean Coast and Galilee

First, some preliminary observations:

Any good tour of the Holy Land should include a reasonable amount of time in the Transjordan. Confining oneself to the area west of the Jordan River, as so many tourists do, results in a fragmented look at the Holy Land which tends to leave a mistaken impression. The character of this land and its history have been shaped as much by the Arabian Desert to the east as by the Mediterranean Sea to the west. Moreover, some of the most interesting scenery and best preserved archaeological sites in the Holy Land are to be found east of the Jordan. These include Jerash, Kerak and Petra. The first two itineraries outlined below originate in Amman and explore the Transjordan.

Most English-speaking tourists visit the Holy Land because it is the land of the Bible. However, it is not only the land of the Bible. People had lived there for thousands of years before the Israelites made their appearance. Historically it is also the land of the Umayyad Caliphs and the Crusaders; more recently it is the land of modern Israel and Jordan. While the itineraries outlined below give full attention to biblical sites and biblical history, a

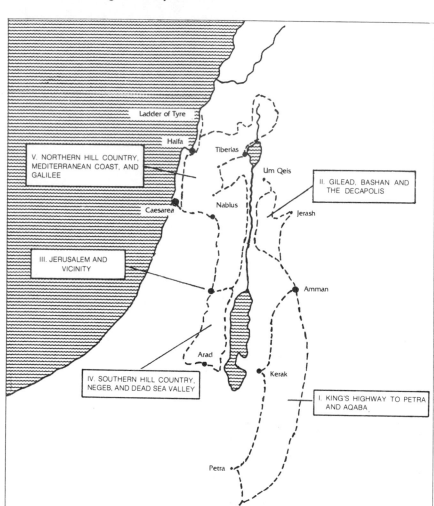

Map 13: FIVE SUGGESTED ITINERARIES

conscious effort has been made to provide a balanced coverage of the entire historical sweep and cultural traditions of the Holy Land.

Finally, a word about so-called traditional sites. Christians, Jews and Moslems have been making religious pilgrimages to the Holy Land for centuries. The primary reason for their coming has been to see the actual places where things mentioned in the Bible and the Koran occurred—the site of Rachel's burial, Jesus' sermon on the Mount, Mohammed's vision of Paradise, and others. Exact locations usually are impossible to determine, however, because the Bible and the Koran do not provide enough specific geographical information. Over the centuries, in an effort to accommodate the pilgrims, traditional sites have been identified where the various events "may have occurred." These traditional sites are not to be ignored; they have become a real part of the history and character of the Holy Land. Still, it is unfortunate that many tours today continue to concentrate on the traditional rather than the authentic archaeological sites. The itineraries suggested below attempt to give a balanced look at both.

Five Suggested Itineraries

The King's Highway to Petra. _____

I find it difficult to imagine a tour of the land of the Bible which does not include Petra. This is almost like visiting Egypt and not seeing the Pyramids. But to try to reach Petra from Amman and then to return in a single day is impractical. Tour groups do this, to be sure, but they manage only by leaving very early in the morning and hurrying to and from Petra along the modern highway which skirts the desert edge. This Desert Highway bypasses many truly interesting places to see in southern Transjordan. Moreover, in attempting to squeeze the trip into a single day, arrival at Petra invariably is late in the morning when it is beginning to get hot; the visit there is necessarily of brief duration, an hour and a half maximum; the return to Amman is boring, back again along the same Desert Highway; and total exhaustion is the result. The road to Petra which follows the route of the old King's Highway (see Map 5 and explanation above) is much more scenic and interesting than the Desert Road. Indeed the sites along the King's Highway deserve a full day of exploration themselves. The best way to see Petra is to spend the night and do your exploring early in the morning while it is still cool and the colors more beautiful. I have found the following travel plan to be quite satisfactory:

- Leave Amman by 8:00 at the latest.
- Follow the King's Highway to Petra and allow the entire day for examining the sites along the way.
- Spend the night at the government rest house at Petra.
- Rise early, spend the full morning exploring Petra and eat a late lunch at the rest house.
- Return to Amman via the Desert Highway (a drive of approximately three and one-half hours).

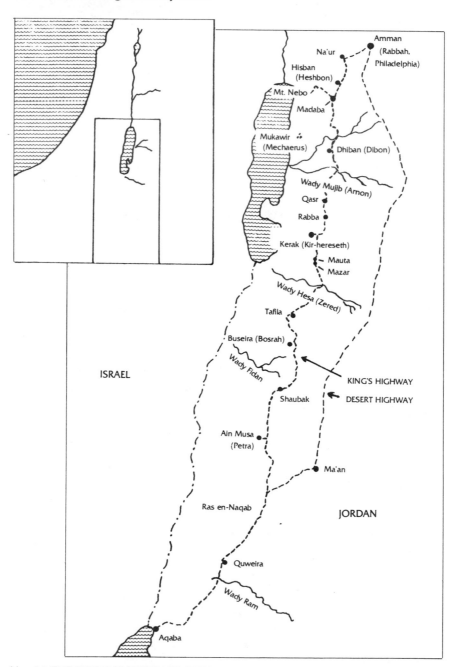

Map 14: THE KING'S HIGHWAY TO PETRA AND AQABA
(For Petra vicinity detail, see p. 72.)

Another option, instead of returning directly to Amman, would be to continue to Aqaba, have a delightful late afternoon swim and spend the night at a beachfront hotel. You can investigate Wady Ram the next morning and return to Amman by mid-afternoon along the Desert Highway. Beginning with Amman, the following points of interest would be covered by this proposed itinerary. Trace the route on Map 14.

Amman. During earliest times, or at least as early as can be determined, this city was known as Rabbah ("chief city" or "capital") of the Ammonites. The Ammonites and Israelites were often at war, and it was during an Israelite siege of Rabbah that David arranged for Uriah's death (see 2 Samuel 11). Other biblical passages which mention the Ammonites are Deuteronomy 3:11; Judges 11; 1 Samuel 11; 2 Samuel 10 and 17:27 and Amos 1:13-15.

Uriah's Death at Rabbah

David's affair with Bathsheba occurred while Israel's armies were besieging Rabbah of the Ammonites (present-day Amman).

> In the spring of the year, the time when kings go forth to battle, David sent Joab, and his servants with him, and all Israel; and they ravaged the Ammonites, and besieged Rabbah. But David remained in Jerusalem. It happened, late one afternoon, when David arose from the couch and was walking upon the roof of the king's house, that he saw from the roof a woman bathing; and the woman was beautiful. . . .

Bathsheba was already married to Uriah, one of the soldiers fighting under Joab. Eventually, as the story unfolds, David decided to arrange for Uriah's death.

> In the morning David wrote a letter to Joab, and sent it by the hand of Uriah. In the letter he wrote, "Set Uriah in the forefront of the hardest fighting, and then draw back from him, that he may be struck down, and die." And as Joab was besieging the city, he assigned Uriah to the place where he knew there would be valiant men. And the men of the city came out and fought with Joab; and some of the servants of David among the people fell. Uriah the Hittite was slain also.

> (2 Samuel 11)

Ptolemy II Philadelphis, one of the Greek rulers who came to power in Egypt after Alexander's conquest, rebuilt Rabbah during the third century B.C. and renamed it Philadelphia. Later, Philadelphia joined the Decapolis League and eventually was annexed to the Roman province of Arabia. In the second century A.D., still under Roman rule, the city was expanded to a grand scale. Philadelphia became the seat of a Bishopric during the Byzantine period and sent representatives to the councils of Nicea (A.D. 325) and Chalcedon (A.D. 451). Although the Umayyads even built a castle on the citadel, the city declined and eventually was left unoccupied during the Arab period.

Roman theater in the heart of modern Amman

Amman's modern history began in 1878 in connection with the Russo-Turkish war. As a consequence of the war, the western slopes of the Caucasus (along the Black Sea coast) fell into Russian hands, producing a flood of "Circassian" refugees. Sultan Abdul Hamid II, the Turkish ruler, resettled some of these Circassians at Amman, as well as at Na'ur, Suweilih and Jerash. Amman still was a small Circassian village in 1921 when Abdullah selected it as administrative center of the newly established Emirate of the Transjordan. It began to grow rapidly; with the flood of Palestinian refugees, especially in 1947-48 and 1967, Amman became a booming metropolis. Today 70-80 percent of Amman's population are first or second generation refugees from the West Bank.

Modern Amman covers a cluster of hills which overlook an upper branch of Nahr ez-Zerka (known in ancient times as the Jabbok river; see below, under "Gilead, Bashan, and the Decapolis"). The most prominent of these hills is the so-called citadel. The area of ancient Rabbah, the city of Old Testament times, was probably confined to this citadel. Ruins of a Roman temple from the time of Marcus Aurelius (A.D. 162-180) and the core of an Umayyad castle are evident there even today. Jordan's national archaeological museum is also located on the citadel, from which point one can survey the modern bustling city, encompassing the remains of other Roman structures, several mosques, and Emir Abdullah's tomb.

Children on a roof in crowded Amman. First and second generation refugees from the West Bank compose most of the city's population.

Na'ur. Take the road from Amman to Na'ur, approximately 10 miles, and then turn south toward Hisban and Madaba. Na'ur is probably the site of biblical Abel-Keramim ("District of the Vineyards"; see Judges 11:33). Between Na'ur and Hisban, on the left (east) side of the road, is a rocky hill today called el-'Al. This is probably the site of biblical Elealeh (see Numbers 32:3, 37; Isaiah 15:4; 16:9).

Hisban. Site of old Heshbon, the capital city of King Sihon, whom the

Israelites are recorded to have defeated on their return from Egypt (Numbers 21). Heshbon is often mentioned in the Old Testament (see especially Isaiah 15-16 and Song of Songs 7:1-5). Herod the Great fortified the site, and it became a flourishing city (called Esbus) in late Roman times. Hisban is a prime example of a "tell," a stratified city ruin; a team of American archaeologists excavated there between 1968 and 1978.

Madaba. This is the site of another ancient city mentioned several times in the Old Testament (Numbers 21:30; 1 Chronicles 19:7) and in the famous Mesha Inscription (see below). Both the Israelites and the Moabites claimed rights to the rich tableland surrounding Madaba—a source of constant friction between these two peoples.

Mosaic map at Madaba with Jerusalem in the lower right corner

Definitely plan a visit to the old church in the middle of the modern village and see the mosaic map. The present church structure dates from 1896, but it was built on the ruins of an older sixth century church. The mosaic floor of this early church is partially preserved and provides a colorful map of the land of the Bible. Because this is the earliest map of the Holy Land in existence, it is extremely useful to geographers and archaeologists.

Madaba is a convenient place for a rest stop. Go to the Madaba Rest House just across and down the street from the church.

Mount Nebo. A secondary road leads from Madaba to a mountain spur overlooking the northeastern end of the Dead Sea. This spur is identified by tradition as Mount Nebo, also called Pisgah, from which Moses viewed the promised land (see Numbers 23:14 and Deuteronomy 32:49). In the fourth century A.D. a church dedicated to Moses was built here. Modified and expanded several times during the next few centuries, it is now being restored by the Franciscan Fathers. Although the exact location of Nebo/Pisgah is uncertain, it must have been somewhere in this area. Moreover, regardless of whether this is the actual Mount Nebo to which the biblical narrative refers, it provides a marvelous view of the Dead Sea and beyond.

Mukawir. Return to Madaba and again head south toward Dhiban. Approximately halfway between Madaba and Dhiban another secondary road leads to Mukawir, the site of ancient Mechaerus, a mountaintop fort of the Hellenistic and Roman periods. Mechaerus was founded by Alexander Jannaeus, one of the Maccabean rulers (103-76 B.C.), destroyed by the Romans in 67 B.C., and rebuilt by Herod the Great. According to Josephus, it was here that Herod Antipas imprisoned and eventually executed John the Baptist. Little remains of the old fort—it was again destroyed by the Romans

---

John the Baptist at Mechaerus

Herod Antipas, who ruled Galilee and part of the Transjordan after the death of Herod the Great, was defeated in a major battle by the Nabateans of Petra. Josephus recorded the event and reports that many of the Jews regarded this as divine punishment because Herod Antipas had executed John the Baptist.

> Now some of the Jews thought that the destruction of Herod's army came from God, and that very justly, as a punishment of what he did against John, that was called "Baptist"; for Herod slew him, who was a good man, and commanded the Jews to exercise virture, both as to righteousness towards one another, and piety toward God. . . . Herod, who feared lest the great influence John had over the people might put it into his power and inclination to raise a rebellion . . ., thought it best, by putting him to death, to prevent any mischief he might cause, and not bring himself into difficulties, by sparing a man who might make him repent of it when it should be too late. Accordingly he was sent a prisoner, out of Herod's suspicious temper, to Machaerus, the castle I mentioned, and was there put to death. Now the Jews had an opinion that the destruction of this army was sent as a punishment upon Herod, as a mark of God's displeasure with him.
>
> (*Antiquities of the Jews* XVIII, 5, 2.)

at the time of the First Jewish Revolt in A.D. 66-70—but the site provides another excellent view of the Dead Sea.

Dhiban. This was ancient Dibon (see Numbers 21:27-30; Isaiah 15:1-9), and the site of the discovery of the famous Mesha Inscription in 1868. This inscription was commissioned by King Mesha, who ruled Moab from Dibon about the same time Jehoram and Jehoshaphat ruled Israel and Judah. Apparently Mesha erected a sanctuary to the Moabite god Chemosh at a place called Qarhoh. Although the inscription was intended primarily to commemorate the completion of that sanctuary, Mesha used the occasion to publicize other major accomplishments of his reign as well. He was especially proud of having recovered the tableland of Madaba from Israel. See above, under "Canaanite Inscriptions," for information about the language and script of the inscription, and below for a full translation. See also 2 Kings 3 for an account of Jehoram's attempt to restore Israelite control over Moab during Mesha's reign.

The Mesha Inscription

In 1868 a German missionary discovered the so-called Mesha Inscription among the ruins of Dibon, an ancient Moabite city. Also called the Moabite Stone, this inscription dates from the reign of King Mesha, mentioned in 2 Kings 3, and is written in the old Canaanite alphabet. It reads as follows (. . . indicates damaged places in the inscription).

I am Mesha, Son of Chemoshyatti, king of Moab, the Dibonite.
My father reigned over Moab thirty years and I reigned after my father.
And I built this sanctuary to Chemosh at Qarhoh . . . because he saved me from
    all the kings and caused me to triumph over all my adversaries.
Omri, king of Israel, oppressed Moab for a long time because Chemosh was
    angry with us.
His son succeeded him and said, "I too will oppress Moab!"
During my reign he said this; but I have triumphed over him and over his house
    and Israel has perished forever.
Omri had occupied the whole land of Madaba and controlled it during his reign
    and during half the reign of his son—forty years. But Chemosh controls it
    during my reign.
And I built Baal-meon, and I made in it a reservoir
And I built Qaryaten
And the men of Gad had dwelt in the land of Ataroth always and the king of Israel
    had fortified Ataroth for them. But I fought against the town and took it. And I
    slew all the people of the town as intoxication for Chemosh and Moab.
And I brought from there the official altar (translation uncertain) and drug it before
    Chemosh at Kerioth. And I settled there (i.e., in Ataroth) men of Sharon and

men of Maharith.

And Chemosh said to me, "Go, take Nebo from Israel." and I went by night and fought against it from the break of dawn until noon. And I took it and I slew all 7,000 men and boys and women and girls and maidservants because I had vowed to sacrifice (literally: devoted them as *herem*) to Ashtar-Chemosh.

And I took from there the official altars (translation uncertain) and drug them before Chemosh.

And the king of Israel built Jahaz and dwelt there while fighting me. But Chemosh drove him out from before me. And I took from Moab 200 men, all of them noblemen, and established them in Jahaz; thus I took possession of it and attached it to the district of Dibon.

And I built Qarhoh, the wall of the forests and the wall of the citadel. And I built its gates and I built its towers. And I built the palace, and I made both of its reservoirs for water inside the town.

And there was no cistern in the town at Qarhoh, and I said to all the people, "Let each of you make a cistern for himself in his house."

And I cut beams for Qarhoh with captives from Israel.

And I built Aroer and I made the highway in the Arnon.

And I built Beth-bamoth for it had been destroyed.

And I built Bezer because it lay in ruins . . .

. . . so men of Dibon, because all Dibon was loyal to me.

And I ruled . . . a hundred towns which I added to the land.

And I built . . . and Beth-diblathen

And I built Beth-baal-meon and placed there . . .

And as for Hauronem, there dwelt in it . . .

. . . Chemosh said to me, "Go down, fight against Hauronem."

And I went down and I fought . . .

. . . Chemosh controlled it during my reign and . . .

Wady Mujib. Soon after passing through the modern village of Dhiban, the edge of Wady Mujib looms. "Wady" is the Arabic word for valley and can denote anything from a small ravine to a major canyon. Wady Mujib is a steep river canyon known in ancient times as the Arnon. Both the Israelites and Moabites claimed the territory north of the Mujib/Arnon, while the plateau south of the Mujib was Moab proper. The modern road across the Mujib follows essentially the route of the old Roman road. Be aware of the Roman milestones along the road, approximately halfway up the southern ascent.

Moab. The Moabite plateau is isolated even today, cut off by the Wady Mujib, the Wady Hesa, the Dead Sea and the desert. But it is fertile land with adequate water supplies. The book of Ruth begins with Naomi's family travelling to Moab in search of food because of famine in Judah. The land of Moab is also exceedingly rich in archaeological remains from virtually every historical period. For example, the modern road skirts temple ruins at Qasr and Rabba, both temples dating from the Roman period.

Isaiah 15: A Pronouncement against Moab

Isaiah 15, a pronouncement against the Moabites of Isaiah's day, provides the names of several ancient Moabite cities and villages.

> Because *Ar* is laid waste in a night Moab is undone;
> because *Kir* is laid waste in a night Moab is undone.
> The daughter of *Dibon* has gone up to the high places to weep;
> over Nebo and over Medeba Moab wails.
> On every head is baldness, every beard is shorn;
> in the streets they gird on sackcloth; on the housetops and in
> the squares every one wails and melts in tears.
> *Heshbon* and *Elealeh* cry out,
> their voice is heard as far as *Jahaz*;
> Therefore the armed men of Moab cry aloud;
> his soul trembles.

The King's Highway passes through the heart of Moab where many of the old village sites are occupied still today. Note how the present-day Arabic names often correspond to the ancient Moabite names.

> Ar = present-day Rabba
> Kir = present-day Kerak
> Dibon = present-day Dhiban
> Medeba = present-day Madaba
> Heshbon = present-day Hisban
> Elealeh = present-day el-Al

The location of ancient Jahaz is no longer known.

Kerak. Situated on a high hill surrounded by steep valleys, Kerak has from earliest times been a key defensive position for the Moabite plateau. This great city was called Kir Moab, and sometimes Kir-heres or Kir-hereseth, during Old Testament times. 2 Kings 3 describes a siege of the city undertaken by the kings of Israel, Judah and Edom. The city almost fell to them, but these three kings decided to withdraw when Mesha sacrificed his oldest son on the city walls.

Called Kharka or Kharkamoba during the Hellenistic, Roman and Byzantine periods, as a Byzantine city it became an important Christian center. The Crusaders built major castles at Kerak and Shaubak, calling them Crac des Moabites and Montreal respectively, and from them dominated the southern Transjordan between ca. 1136 and 1188. The last Crusader lord of Kerak was the infamous Renaud de Chatillon, whose attacks on Muslim pilgrims angered Saladin and led to the decisive battle at the Horns of Hattin in 1187. Saladin was victorious at Hattin and personally executed Renaud on the spot. Kerak fell the following year.

Kerak Castle

The government rest house at Kerak is a good place for lunch—although by the time you get there it will have to be a rather late lunch. Allow at least an hour after lunch for exploring the old castle.

Mauta and Mazar. These twin villages are situated seven and eight miles south of Kerak, respectively. The first clash between the Islamic forces and those of Byzantium occurred near Mauta in A.D. 629. The Islamic forces were defeated; three of the Arabic leaders were killed and are buried in the Mosque at Mazar.

Wady Hesa. Although its sides are not as steep, this second river canyon is as massive as the Mujib and takes as long to cross. Wady Hesa is probably the Zered of Old Testament times (See Numbers 21:12; Deuteronomy 2:13). If so, then by crossing the Hesa one enters the territory of ancient Edom. Located atop a steep hill in the middle of the canyon is Khirbet et-Tannur, a Nabatean temple now in ruins.

Edom. The Israelites considered the Edomites both close relations, as descendants of Esau, and hated enemies (read Numbers 20:14-21; Amos 1:11-12; Jeremiah 49:7-22; and Obadiah). In Hellenistic and Roman times this area south of Wady Hesa was occupied by the Nabateans.

Buseira. This little Arab village is atop the ruins of old Bozrah, the chief city of the Edomites (see Amos 1:11-12; Isaiah 34:5-12, especially verse 6:63:1; and Jeremiah 49:13, 22). The British School of Archaeology excavated the site from 1971 to 1980 and uncovered remains of massive buildings from Edomite times.

References to Bozrah in the Hebrew Prophets

Bozrah, chief city of the Edomites, was an important city during Old Testament times. Consider the following passages from the prophets:

Thus says the LORD:
"For three transgressions of Edom, and for four, I will not revoke the
    punishment,
because he pursued his brother with the sword, and cast off all pity,
and his anger tore perpetually, and he kept his wrath forever.
So I will send a fire upon Teman, and it shall devour the strongholds
    of *Bozrah*,"

(Amos 1:11-12)

Who is this that comes from Edom,
    in crimsoned garments from *Bozrah*,
he that is glorious in his apparel,
    marching in the greatness of his strength.

(Isaiah 63:1)

Behold, one shall mount up and fly swiftly like an eagle,
and spread his wings against *Bozrah*, and the heart of
the warriors of Edom shall be in that day like the heart
of a woman in her pangs.

(Jeremiah 49:22)

Wady Dana. Stop and enjoy the scenic view from the point where the road passes along the edge of Wady Dana. Further to the west this wady joins Wady Fidan, "Punon" of Old Testament times (see Numbers 33:42-43). The ancients worked copper mines in Punon.

Shaubak. The Crusaders selected this location for their castle, Montreal, built in 1115. Montreal fell to Saladin in 1188. Rebuilt by the Mamluks in the fourteenth century, it was again almost totally demolished by Ibrahim Pasha in 1832. The castle ruins are difficult to reach, but a fantastic view of them is possible from a point accessible by a secondary paved road.

Petra. On approaching Petra, one of the first landmarks is a copious spring which the Arabs call Ain Musa, or "Spring of Moses." Tradition holds that this was the spring Moses produced upon striking the rock (see Numbers 20). Associated with Ain Musa is Wady Musa, a usually dry river bed which works its way westward to the Arabah. But during heavy rains it becomes a rushing torrent and in the course of geological time has cut a deep, narrow passage through the red (Nubian) sandstone between Ain Musa and the Arabah. This narrow passage, called the "sik," opens into a broad isolated valley where once flourished the Nabatean-Roman city of Petra.

el-Deir ("the Monestary") at Petra

Within the valley itself is a huge rock formation on which archaeologists have found Iron Age remains. This rock formation is called Um el-Biyara, and some scholars identify it as Edomite Sela, mentioned in the Old Testament (2 Kings 14:7). Sela means "rock" in Hebrew, and Petra means "rock" in Greek.

It was under the Nabateans, however, that Petra achieved its golden age and eventually covered the entire valley. In addition to the impressive city which filled the valley, the Nabateans carved hundreds of chambers with elegant facades into the stone cliffs surrounding their city. The city is no more, but the carved chambers, most of them intended as tombs, remain. Nabatea fell increasingly under Roman influence after the middle of the first century B.C., and by A.D. 106 all southern Transjordan had been incorporated into the Roman Empire and designated as the province of Arabia Petraea. Petra continued to flourish for yet another hundred years but began to decline in the third century A.D.

The archaeological remains at Petra are truly spectacular, but it is the natural beauty of the place that makes Petra one of the all time wonders of the world. The beauty is indescribable; it is a personal experience.

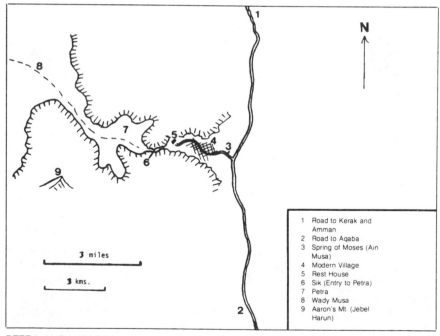

N

	1	Road to Kerak and Amman
	2	Road to Aqaba
	3	Spring of Moses (Ain Musa)
	4	Modern Village
	5	Rest House
	6	Sik (Entry to Petra)
	7	Petra
	8	Wady Musa
	9	Aaron's Mt. (Jebel Harun)

3 miles

3 kms.

PETRA AND VICINITY

Aqaba. The drive from Petra back to Amman via the Desert Highway takes approximately three and a half hours. But why not continue to Aqaba? Allow two hours and a half for the drive and plan for a refreshing swim upon arrival.

The Red Sea at Aqaba

Aqaba and Elat are twin cities on the Red Sea, situated on the Jordanian and Israeli sides of the border, respectively. Ancient Ezion-geber was probably in this vicinity (Deuteronomy 2:8; 1 Kings 22:48). The Crusaders built a small fortress at Aqaba which was expanded during the fourteenth and fifteenth centuries. The Arabs seized Aqaba from the Turks during World War I and used its harbor as an important supply base.

The Desert Highway. It is a direct path from Aqaba back to Amman on the Desert Highway. Skirting the edge of the desert, this road follows the route of the old Darb el-Hajj ("Pilgrim's Road") by which Muslim pilgrims journeyed from Damascus to Mecca before commercial airplanes. The Ottoman government even established rest stations along the way, the one at Qatrana still standing and visible from the highway. The railway paralleling the road north of Ma'an was also built by the Turks and originally connected Damascus with Medina.

Wady Ram. A recently paved secondary road leads from the Desert Highway into Wady Ram as far as a Desert Patrol police station. This is a diversion well worth the time. Stop at the police station, and chances are local Bedouin will soon appear offering camel rides for appropriate remuneration. If you have never ridden a camel, here is your chance.

A
camel
ride
in
Wady
Ram

Gilead, Bashan, and the Decapolis

Northern Transjordan was known as Gilead and Bashan in Old Testament times. During the Roman period certain of the cities in this area joined together to form a league, known as the Decapolis league because they were approximately ten in number. Correspondingly, it became common practice to refer to the entire northern Transjordan as the Decapolis (Matthew 4:25). Roman and Byzantine ruins still stand in several of the Decapolis cities: Philadelphia (present-day Amman), Gerasa (Jerash), Pella (Fahl) and

Bedouin
tent
in
Wady
Ram

Gadara (Um Qeis). An added attraction in northern Transjordan is Nahr ez-Zerqa. This was the Old Testament Jabbok River, on whose banks Jacob wrestled with the angel (Genesis 32). I suggest a full day excursion into Gilead, Bashan and the Decapolis area with the itinerary outlined below. It begins with a drive into the Jordan Valley by way of the modern cities of Suweilih and es-Salt. Follow the route on Map 15.

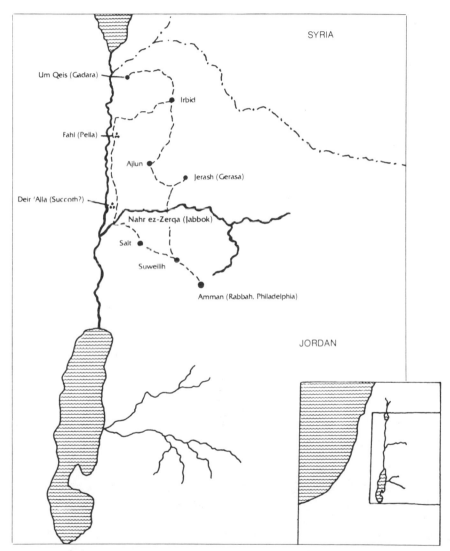

SYRIA

Um Qeis (Gadara)

Irbid

Fahl (Pella)

Ajlun

Jerash (Gerasa)

Deir 'Alla (Succoth?)

Nahr ez-Zerqa (Jabbok)

Salt

Suweilih

Amman (Rabbah, Philadelphia)

JORDAN

Map 15: GILEAD, BASHAN, AND THE DECAPOLIS

Suweilih. Settled by Circassians in 1878 (see above, under "Amman"), Suweilih is so rapidly expanding alongside Amman that soon their city limits will meet.

es-Salt. This was the chief administrative center in the Transjordan during the Turkish period. There was even some consideration in 1921 to making it, instead of Amman, the capitol of the Emirate of the Transjordan. Es-Salt, whose name comes from the Latin *saltus*, meaning "wooded valley," traces its history back at least to the Roman period. It was fortified by the Mamluks and destroyed by the Mongols. Later rebuilt, it was again destroyed, this time by Ibrahim Pasha.

The Jordan Valley. West of es-Salt the road descends into the Jordan Valley—stop and enjoy the view. At one point you can see as far as Ebal and Gerizim, the twin mountains which overlook Nablus (ancient Shechem; see Map 6, above).

Tell Deir 'Alla and Tell es-Sa'idiyeh. Several "tells" are obvious on both sides of the main road leading northward through the Jordan Valley. Tell Deir 'Alla, associated with ancient Succoth (Joshua 13:27; Judges 8:5-9, 14-16; 1 Kings 7:46; Psalms 60:6), is being excavated by a Dutch archaeological team. Already they have discovered a Late Bronze Age temple and fragments of an Iron Age plaster wall exhibiting Aramaic script. Although poorly preserved, the text clearly alludes to a prophet named Balaam (see Numbers 22:5-24:25).

Tell es-Sa'idiyeh, a few miles further north and on the same side of the main road, is believed by some scholars to be biblical Zarethan (Joshua 3:16; 1 Kings 7:46). An American team, excavating there between 1964 and 1967, uncovered stratified city remains from the Early Bronze, Late Bronze and Early Iron Ages.

Fahl (Pella). A major city stood at this beautiful, well-watered spot during the Bronze Age. It is mentioned several times in contemporary Egyptian records, where it is called Pihilu or Pelel. For example, the Amarna Letters (above, under "Cuneiform Texts from Mesopotamia") include one piece of correspondence from "Mut-Ba'lu, the prince of Pelel." Nothing is known of the city during Old Testament times, but it later emerged as an important city, known as Pella, and thrived during the Hellenistic, Roman and Byzantine periods. It was one of the Decapolis cities of the Roman period.

According to Eusebius, a 4th century Bishop of Caesarea who wrote a history of the Church, the Christians in Jerusalem fled to Pella at the time of the First Jewish Revolt (A.D. 66-70). In the Late Roman and Byzantine periods Pella became a strong Christian center. Fahl/Pella is an exceedingly rich archaeological site excavated on numerous occasions by teams representing various nationalities.

Christians Flee from Jerusalem to Pella

The Christian church was still in its infancy at the time of the First Jewish Revolt in A.D. 66-70. According to Eusebius, a fourth century bishop of Caesarea, the Christians abandoned Jerusalem at that time and fled to Pella.

> After Nero had held the government about thirteen years, Galba and Otho reigned about a year and six months. Vespasian, who had become illustrious in the campaign against the Jews, was then proclaimed sovereign in Judea, receiving the title of emperor from the armies there. Directing his course, therefore, immediately to Rome, he commits the care of the war against the Jews, into the hands of his son Titus; for after the ascension of our Savior, the Jews, in addition to their wickedness against him, were now incessantly plotting mischief against his apostles. . . .The whole (Christian) body, however, the church of Jerusalem, having been commanded by divine revelation, given to men of approved piety there before the war, removed from the city, and dwelt at a certain town beyond the Jordan, called Pella. Here, those that believed in Christ, having removed from Jerusalem, as if holy men had entirely abandoned the royal city itself, and the whole land of Judea; the divine justice, for their crimes against Christ and his apostles, finally overtook them, totally destroying the whole generation of these evildoers from the earth.
>
> (*Ecclesiastical History* Book III, Ch. 5)

Um Qeis (Gadara). The ruins of this once magnificent city cover the edge of a plateau overlooking the Sea of Galilee. Known as Gadara, but not the Gadara of the Gadarine swine incident, this ancient city flourished during the Hellenistic-Roman-Byzantine periods. Antiochus III took it from the Ptolemys in 218 B.C.; Alexander Jannaeus added it to his kingdom in 98 B.C.; Pompey conquered it in 63 B.C. Gadara eventually became one of the Decapolis cities and produced a number of philosophers and poets, including Philodemus, an Epicurean philosopher from the first century A.D., Meleager, a poet from the same century, and Menippus, a satirist from the third century. The city had its martyrs as well, among them Zachary, a deacon of Gadara who was beheaded during Diocletian's reign. Later, in

Byzantine times, Gadara became the seat of a Bishopric and remained important until the Arab invasion.

Irbid. This rapidly expanding city, built over an ancient ruin, dates back to the Early Bronze Age. Quite possibly it is the site of ancient Beth Arbel (Hosea 10:14). The old name survived in Roman-Byzantine Arbela, represented by Tell Abil, located only a few miles north of Irbid.

Rabad Castle. Near the busy city of Ajlun, on a high hill with a commanding view, stands Rabad castle. Built originally in 1184-85 by one of Saladin's governors, and cousin, it protected the northern Transjordan against Crusader expansion. Later (1214-15) it was enlarged by the Ayyubids and was even held for a short time (in 1260) by the Mongols. Although the castle itself is difficult to reach from the main road, the view from the edifice is breathtaking.

Jerash (Gerasa). On a branch of Wady Jerash, this site was ideal for habitation in ancient times. But while archaeological remains from the Neolithic and Early Bronze Ages have been found in the immediate vicinity, it was only during the Hellenistic period that a major city emerged. The Hellenistic city was "Antioch on the Chrysorrhoas." Chrysorrhoas means "Golden River"; the name "Antioch" suggests that it had been founded by one of the Seleucid rulers who favored Antiochus as a dynastic name. It was during the Roman period, however, especially during the second century A.D., that the city reached its zenith. It was known as Gerasa at that time, and most of the ruins visible at the site today date from the second century.

Gerasa was one of several cities which depended heavily on trade between the Roman empire and Arabia. Others were Baalbek (in Lebanon), Bostra (in Syria) and Petra. The eastern trade routes began to shift in the third century, introducing a period of decline for these cities. Gerasa continued its existence throughout the Byzantine period, boasting numerous Christian churches; but its heyday clearly was past. Eventually, in the Arab period, it ceased to be occupied.

Gerasa (Jerash in Arabic) is one of the best-preserved examples of a provincial Roman city in existence. Its unusually fine state of preservation is due to its location on the desert fringe, somewhat "off the beaten track." But the ruins do reflect changes which have occurred since Roman times. In addition to the general destruction resulting from ravages of time (1) many of the pagan temples were converted to Byzantine churches; (2) the Umayyad caliph Yazid II had the mosaic floors of most of the churches destroyed in 740 A.D. because they were considered idolatrous; (3) the temple of Artemis was converted to a fort and badly damaged by struggles between Crusaders

Jerash

and Damascus rulers; and finally, (4) Jerash was resettled by Circassians in 1878, who reused much of the stone from the Roman buildings for their own houses.

Beginning with John Garstang, who excavated there in 1925, Jerash has attracted an almost constant stream of archaeologists. Excavations and reconstruction are underway even now, sponsored by the Jordan Department of Antiquities.

Key Events in the History of Jerash

- Settlements on this spot as early as the Neolithic and Early Bronze Periods.
- Emerges as an important city during the Hellenistic period, at which time it was called Antioch on the Chrysorrhoas.
- Conquered by Alexander Jannaeus (103-76 B.C.) and annexed to the Maccabean kingdom of Jerusalem.
- Liberated from Maccabean control by Pompey in 63 B.C., at which time it joined with certain other cities, most of them clustered in the northern Transjordan, to form the Decapolis League. By this time its name had changed to Gerasa.
- A.D. 90, the whole northern Transjordan, including Gerasa, is incorporated into the Roman province of Arabia.
- The Roman Emperor Trajan (A.D. 98-117) paves with stones and fortifies the old trade route which connected Damascus with Aqaba and Arabia. Possibly this route is to be identified with the King's Highway of Old Testament times; now it comes to be called the Via Nova. Gerasa, situated on the Via Nova, became exceedingly wealthy during the second century A.D.

from the trade which passed along this highway.
- Triumphal arch erected in A.D. 129-30 to commemorate the Roman Emperor Hadrian's visit to the city. Most of the other ruins which one sees at Jerash today also date from the second century (the temple of Artemis, the temple of Zeus, the Nymphaeum, the theater).
- Eastern trade routes begin to shift during the third century A.D., primarily as a result of the emergence of the Sassanian kingdom in Mesopotamia. Gerasa is promoted to the rank of Roman colony, but begins a steady decline.
- Declining Gerasa becomes a Christian city during the Byzantine period, at which time it boasted numerous churches.

Nahr ez-Zerqa. Proceeding northward through the Jordan Valley, you crossed the River Zerqa (Nahr means "river" in Arabic). You now cross it further upstream, a better place to stop. As indicated above, the Zerqa was called the Jabbok in Old Testament times. Somewhere along its banks stood a sanctuary known as Penuel which marked the spot where Jacob wrestled with the angel (Genesis 32:31; Judges 8:8-9; 1 Kings 12:25). A city named Mahanaim (Genesis 32:2; 2 Samuel 17-18) was in the same general vicinity. The exact locations of Penuel and Mahanaim have not been determined.

Jerusalem and Vicinity

It will not be very useful to suggest a specific itinerary for exploring Jerusalem and vicinity because the points of interest are in such close proximity. I propose here to note only some of the most important landmarks. More detailed information will be provided in Part Three, under "More about Jerusalem."

Street
scene
in
Eastern
Jerusalem

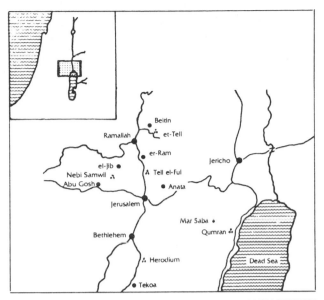

Map 16: JERUSALEM AND VICINITY

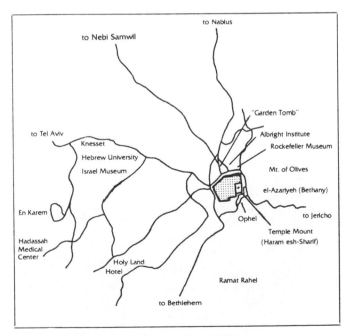

Map 17: JERUSALEM: METROPOLITAN AREA

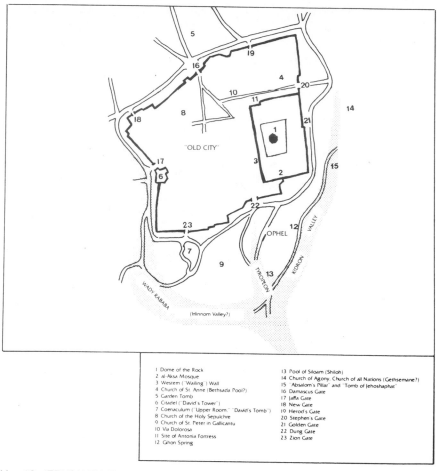

1 Dome of the Rock
2 al-Aksa Mosque
3 Western ("Wailing") Wall
4 Church of St. Anne (Bethsada Pool?)
5 Garden Tomb
6 Citadel ("David's Tower")
7 Coenaculum ("Upper Room," "David's Tomb")
8 Church of the Holy Sepulchre
9 Church of St. Peter in Gallicantu
10 Via Dolorosa
11 Site of Antonia Fortress
12 Gihon Spring

13 Pool of Siloam (Shiloh)
14 Church of Agony. Church of all Nations (Gethsemane?)
15 "Absalom's Pillar" and "Tomb of Jehoshaphat"
16 Damascus Gate
17 Jaffa Gate
18 New Gate
19 Herod's Gate
20 Stephen's Gate
21 Golden Gate
22 Dung Gate
23 Zion Gate

Map 18: JERUSALEM: The "OLD CITY" and "OPHEL"

The Temple Mount/Haram esh-Sharif. That part of Jerusalem within the Turkish walls is generally referred to as the "Old City." See Maps 17 and 18. The rectangular enclosure in the southeastern corner of the Old City is called the Temple Mount by Jews and Christians and Haram esh-Sharif ("the Noble Sanctuary") by Arabs. The Dome of the Rock monument and the al-Aksa Mosque occupy this enclosure today; in Jesus' day the Jewish Temple stood there. More than likely the Solomonic temple was located on this spot during Old Testament times. The rock outcropping covered by the Dome of the Rock monument is traditionally thought to be the place Abraham brought Isaac for sacrifice and where Mohammed had his vision of paradise.

Walls of Jerusalem at the "Golden Gate"

Ophel. This long sloping hill immediately south of the Temple Mount/ Haram esh-Sharif is the site of oldest Jerusalem, the Bronze Age City which David conquered. Although only Ophel was fortified during the Bronze Age and David's reign, it is completely outside the city walls today. Evidently Solomon expanded the city beyond Ophel to include a portion of the Temple

Mount. The city was further expanded under later Judean kings to encompass a portion of the hill immediately west of that same spot. Eventually, by the Late Roman Period, the city fortifications had shifted still further so as to leave Ophel completely outside the city walls.

During Hezekiah's reign, a tunnel was engineered to bring water from the spring of Gihon to the pool of Siloam. Gihon is situated at the foot of Ophel on the east and would have been outside the city wall; Siloam, on the southwestern slope of Ophel, would have been inside the wall at that time. The purpose of the tunnel, therefore, was to insure a water supply inside the city in case of enemy attack. This same pool of Siloam, into which the water flows from the tunnel, is mentioned in the New Testament. According to John 9:1-12, Jesus sent the blind man, whom he had healed with spit-clay, to wash in this pool.

Hezekiah's Tunnel

The account of King Hezekiah's reign in 2 Chronicles 29-32 includes the following note. See specifically verse 32:30.

> This same Hezekiah closed the upper outlet of the waters of Gihon and directed them down to the west side of the city of David.

Water still flows through an ancient tunnel which connects the spring of Gihon with the Pool of Siloam. In 1880 an old inscription was discovered in the tunnel. The inscription was in Hebrew, written with the old Canaanite alphabet. Unfortunately it was badly damaged before scholars had a chance to study it. The broken text reads as follows:

> . . . the tunneling through. And this is the account of the tunneling through. While [the workmen raised] the pick each toward his fellow and while there [remained] to be tunneled [through, there was heard] the voice of a man calling to his fellow, for there was a split in the rock on the right hand and on [the left hand]. And on the day of the tunneling through the workmen stuck, each in the direction of his fellow, pick against pick. And the water started flowing from the source to the pool, twelve hundred cubits. And the height of the rock above the head of the workmen was a hundred cubits.

It seems reasonable to conclude that this old tunnel which connects Gihon with the Pool of Siloam is Hezekiah's tunnel and that the inscription dates from Hezekiah's reign (715-687 B.C.).

The Church of the Holy Sepulchre. Commissioned in A.D. 326 by the Emperor Constantine, this church has been built, re-built, modified and restored time and again. What were originally two adjacent churches marking the traditional locations of Jesus' crucifixion (Golgotha) and burial (Joseph of Arimathea's tomb), have been contained under one roof since the Crusades. Whether the Church of the Holy Sepulchre actually is the authentic site of Jesus' crucifixion and burial is disputed by scholars (see under "More about Jerusalem," in Part Three, below). Indisputably, this old church is a genuine and most interesting historical place in its own right. For almost seventeen centuries its walls have stood, looming high above the heads of devout Christians on meaningful pilgrimages.

The walk through the narrow streets of the Old City to the Church is a delightful experience; sights, sounds and smells will be remembered and enjoyed for many years.

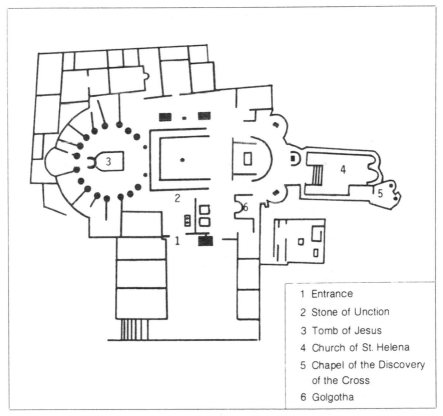

1 Entrance

2 Stone of Unction

3 Tomb of Jesus

4 Church of St. Helena

5 Chapel of the Discovery
  of the Cross

6 Golgotha

CHURCH OF THE HOLY SEPULCHRE

Mount Zion. The Old Testament writers so closely associated Solomon's temple with Mount Zion that it is tempting to suppose that indeed it was Zion on which the temple stood (see Psalms 2 and 132). But in later sources, and continuing today, the name Zion is associated with the hill at the southwest corner of the Old City and not with Temple Mount. According to tradition, David's tomb, the "Upper Room," the house of Caiphas, and the house where the apostles gathered on the day of Pentecost were all located on this southwestern hill.

Mount Scopus and the Mount of Olives. Separated from Jerusalem by the Kidron Valley, these two prominent mountain ridges provide an excellent view of the city from the northeast and east respectively. Mount Scopus to the northeast may be the Nob mentioned in Isaiah 10:32. David is reported to

---

Jerusalem, a Holy City for Three Faiths

Jewish, Christian and Muslim pilgrims have made their way to Jerusalem through the ages, the focus of their attention being three holy spots surprisingly near to each other. Jews come to pray at the Western Wall (sometimes called the Wailing Wall), which is a remnant of the Jewish temple compound of the Roman period. Specifically, it is a remnant of the retaining wall which surrounded the so-called Second Temple—the temple which was built after the exile, lavishly expanded by Herod the Great, and destroyed by Titus in A.D. 70. This is the temple which Jesus would have known.

Christian pilgrims collect not far away at the Church of the Holy Sepulchre which covers the traditional site of Jesus' crucifixion and burial. This church has undergone numerous modifications since it was founded in A.D. 326. The building itself is an archaeological marvel.

Muslims pray at the Dome of the Rock and al-Aksa Mosque, both within the old temple area. Al-Aksa means "the distant place" in Arabic. According to Muslim tradition this is the distant place to which Mohammed was transported in a dream and received a vision of paradise. The Dome of the Rock monument was built by an Umayyad Caliph, Abd el-Malik (A.D. 685-705). The al-Aksa Mosque was built by Abd el-Malik's son, al-Walid (705-715).

have fled Jerusalem across the Mount of Olives at the time of Absalom's rebellion (2 Samuel 15:30). Jesus spent the night on the Mount of Olives, or possibly at nearby Bethany, during his last week in Jerusalem (Luke 21:37).

Nebi Samwil, a mountain further to the northwest of Jerusalem, is another historic vantage point. In earlier days, when pilgrims approached Jerusalem on foot or by horseback from the sea coast, this mountain provided their first view of the city. Usually they camped there overnight, actually arriving in Jerusalem the following day. Nebi Samwil means "Prophet Samuel" in Arabic, reflecting a traditional belief that on this mountain Samuel was buried.

The "Garden Tomb"

Rockefeller and Israel Museums. The Rockefeller Museum, just outside the northeast corner of the Old City walls, was the archaeological museum for Palestine during the mandate period. Artifacts from excavations conducted prior to the mid-1940s are displayed in chronological order. Some materials have been added since the 1940s, but most of the later artifacts are in either the Israel Museum near the Knesset building or the Jordan Museum in Amman. A special feature of the Israel Museum is the Shrine of the Book, a building designed specifically to house the Dead Sea Scrolls.

The Holy Land Hotel is not exactly a museum, but it deserves mention in the same context. The late Professor Michael Avi-Yonah constructed on the premises a 1:50 scale model of Jerusalem as it looked at the time of Herod Agrippa. Though much of the reconstruction is hypothetical, it is based on the latest archaeological evidence.

Hadassah Medical Center. No trip to Jerusalem is complete without a visit to the synagogue of the Hadassah Medical Center. Here are Marc Chagall's famous stained glass windows, twelve panels in brilliant colors, and each focusing on one of the twelve tribes of Israel.

The Southern Hill Country, Negeb and Dead Sea Valley

One of the most interesting aspects of the Holy Land is the variety of topographical and climatic zones found within its small area. This will be especially apparent on an excursion through the hill country south of Jerusalem, across the Negeb, and back through the Dead Sea Valley. There are also some very important historical and archaeological sites along this route. I suggest a two-day excursion including an overnight stay at Arad. Follow the route on Map 19.

Ramat Rahel, Rachel's Tomb. Genesis 35:16-20 recounts Jacob's burial of Rachel near a place called Ephrath. Ephrath is generally equated with Bethlehem (although not without some question), and approximately midway between Jerusalem and Bethlehem is a prominent hill known as Ramat-Rahel, which means the "hill (or height) of Rachel." Nearby, where the road from Jerusalem reaches the outskirts of Bethlehem, is the traditional site of Rachel's tomb. Archaeological excavations at Ramat Rahel have revealed an imposing structure which stood there in the days of the Judean kings, possibly the royal estate alluded to in Jeremiah 22:13-19.

Church
of the
Nativity
as seen by
David
Roberts
in 1838

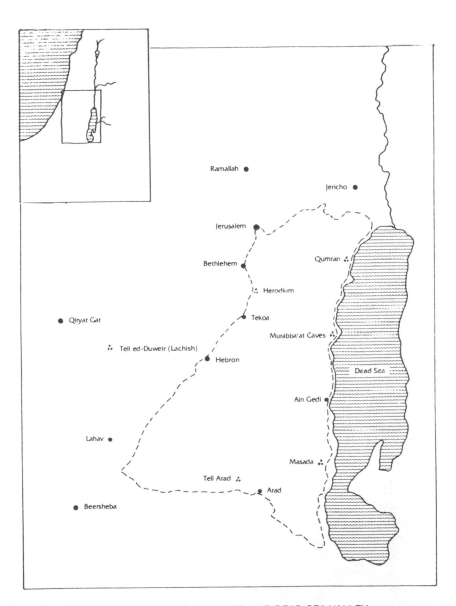

Map 19: SOUTHERN HILL COUNTRY, NEGEB AND DEAD SEA VALLEY

Bethlehem. Although only a small village before 1948, Bethlehem has played an important part in religious history for three interrelated reasons: (1) It was King David's ancestral home (read Ruth; 1 Samuel 16; 2 Samuel 23). (2) It was the place of Jesus' birth, his parents having returned there for a census because Joseph was "of the house and lineage of David" (Matthew 2:1-16; Luke 2:4-15). (3) In A.D. 330, Constantine founded the Church of the Nativity above the traditional birthplace of Jesus. Since then, this church has been an important ecclesiastical and pilgrimage center. According to Jerome, who resided at Bethlehem in the fourth century and translated the Vulgate there, a grove sacred to Tammuz (Adonis) shaded the tomb area (actually a cave) during the two centuries between Hadrian's reign and the founding of the church.

The Church of the Nativity, like the Church of the Holy Sepulchre in Jerusalem, has been restored and modified innumerable times. Roman Catholics (represented by the Franciscans), Greek Orthodox and Armenian Orthodox share traditional rights to the sanctuary, but not always on a friendly basis. For example, a conflict between the Franciscan and Greek Orthodox priests was one of the contributing factors to the outbreak of the

---

Highlights in the History of the Church of the Nativity

• Founded by Constantine in A.D. 330; dedicated by Helena, Constantine's mother, in 339. The fragment of Mosaic floor preserved beneath the present floor probably belonged to this original church.

• Extensive repairs and additions by the Emperor Justinian (527-565). The nave and Corinthian columns date from this building phase.

• Spared by the Persian invaders in 614, apparently because of the mosaics on the interior walls. These mosaics depict the Wise Men, whom the Persian soldiers associated with their own priests. Most of the other Christian churches in the Holy Land were destroyed at that time.

• Restored by the Crusaders. The grey marble slab floor dates from the Crusader period.

• Entrance reduced in size during the Mamluk period to prevent entry into the sanctuary on horseback.

• Conflict between the Franciscans and Greek Orthodox priests contributes to the outbreak of the Crimean war (1854-56).

Crimean War (1854-56). The Franciscans were supported by France, the Greek Orthodox by Russia.

Luke 2:8-20 describes an appearance of angels to shepherds who, at the time of Jesus' birth, were keeping their flocks somewhere in the vicinity of Bethlehem. Three different spots are pointed out today, each claiming to be the place where the angels appeared.

The Herodium. Herod the Great built a fort on top of this steep, isolated mountain at the edge of the Judean Wilderness. Situated opposite the Dead Sea from Mechaerus (see above, under "Mukawir") and within sight of Jerusalem, the fort has a double circular defensive wall strengthened by four towers. Josephus contends that Herod was buried in the fort, but excavations have not yet revealed a tomb.

Tekoa. The road from the Herodium to Hebron passes Taqu'a, an Arab village. Undoubtedly this is the site of ancient Tekoa, best known as the home of the prophet Amos. It was also the home of Ira, one of David's mighty men, and of an anonymous woman who figured in the conflict between David and Absalom (2 Samuel 13:37-14:24; 23:26).

Hebron. According to Numbers 13:22, Hebron was founded even before Zoan (Tanis), an ancient city in the Egyptian delta. It is sacred to Jews, Arabs and Christians alike because of its association with the patriarchs, primarily Abraham. We read in Genesis that Abraham pitched his tent at the Oaks of Mamre near Hebron and purchased the Cave of Machpelah, also nearby, for family burials. Arab tradition emphasizes Abraham's role as the friend of God (Allah); accordingly, their name for Hebron is el-Khalil, or "the friend." Herod the Great built a massive structure over a cave here, traditionally identified as Machpelah. This Herodian structure still stands, having been converted to a mosque during the Arab period.

The ancient city of Hebron was probably confined to Jabel el-Rumeida, a hill overlooking the modern city. Excavations on Jebel el-Remeida in 1966 revealed Bronze Age and Iron Age occupations. David would have known the Iron Age city. He was crowned king at Hebron and ruled there seven and a half years before conquering Jerusalem (2 Samuel 5:1-11). Always politically active, the people at Hebron would later support Absalom's revolt. Hebron has been the scene of political unrest in recent times as well. Hebron and Nablus have been centers of Arab resistance to Israel's occupation of the West Bank.

The Shephelah and Negeb. Hebron is situated in the heart of the southern hill country, which is rugged but well-watered and fertile terrain.

Both to the west and south this rugged terrain is transformed into gradually sloping hills. Lowlands to the west, which give way in turn to the coastal plain, are called the Shephelah. Those to the south represent the desert fringe, or the Negeb. Some of the oldest cities of the Holy Land were located in the Shephelah and Negeb; their stratified ruins ("tells") are providing archaeologists with a wealth of information about life in ancient times. Among the old tells in the Shephelah are Tell el-Rumeileh (biblical Beth Shemesh: 1 Samuel 6; 2 Kings 14:11-13), Tell es-Safi (possibly biblical Gath: Joshua 11:22, 1 Samuel 7:4-23) and Tell ed-Duweir (possibly biblical Lachish: Joshua 10:32; 2 Kings 14:19). Among those in the Negeb are Tell es-Seba (biblical Beersheba: Judges 20:1; 1 Samuel 8:1-2; Amos 5:5), Tell el-Milh (possibly biblical Hormah: Numbers 14:45; Judges 1:17) and Tell Arad (biblical Arad; Numbers 21:1-3; Judges 1:16). Plan to visit one or two of these old tells. If possible, visit one while archaeological excavations are underway.

Tell Arad. Tell Arad is one of the most easily accessible and provocative of these old tells. Excavations between 1962-67 revealed Arad as a major walled city during the Early Bronze Age which was deserted approximately 2000 B.C. and remained a desolate ruin for the next thousand years. Then, in the period of the Israelite Judges, a new settlement emerged on the site. Eventually it was fortified, possibly by Solomon, and served as one of several forts protecting Judah's southern border until the kingdom's destruction by the Babylonians in the sixth century B.C.. The excavators discovered an Israelite sanctuary inside the fort and numerous ostraca (potsherds with

---

Ostraca from Arad

Excavations at several biblical sites in the Holy Land have produced ostraca, sherds of jars on which records or messages are written. At Tell Arad, for example, archaeologists uncovered more than two hundred Hebrew and Aramaic ostraca. Only a small percentage of these were sufficiently preserved to be read. Some of the Arad ostraca date from the last years of the kingdom of Judah and were addressed to one Eliashib, commander of the military garrison at Arad. One of these apparently refers to the temple of Yahweh in Jerusalem.

> To my Lord Eliashib, may Yahweh grant thy welfare! And (as) of now, give Shemariah half an aroura (of grain?) and to Kerosi give a quarter aroura and to the sanctuary (give) what thou didst recommend to me. As for Shallum, he shall stay at the Temple of Yahweh.

writing on them). Several of these ostraca were letters sent to the garrison commander of Arad approximately 600 B.C.

Arad is being developed as a national park designed to provide an overview of the relationship between the Bronze Age and Iron Age phases of the city. Remains from later periods were discovered at Tell Arad also— Persian, Hellenistic, Roman, Arab—but these were not as extensive as those of the Bronze and Iron Ages. The modern city of Arad is about 10 miles eastward.

The Judean Wilderness. Between the central hill country and the Dead Sea are the "bad lands" of Palestine. Known during biblical times as the Judean Wilderness, this rugged, dry, thinly populated area was an ideal sanctuary for outlaws and rebels. David and his soldiers roamed the Judean Wilderness while avoiding Saul. Jewish rebels retreated there when the First Jewish Revolt (A.D. 66-70) and the Bar-Kochba Revolt (A.D. 132-135) were crushed.

Having driven south from Jerusalem to the Negeb through the central hill country, it is now appropriate to return via the Wilderness. A paved highway skirts the Dead Sea.

Masada. This is the largest and most famous of Herod the Great's mountaintop fortifications. The mountain is an isolated rock with steep sides. Herod encircled the crest of the rock with a double wall, constructed cisterns and storehouses to insure an almost inexhaustible water and food supply, and built an impressive three-level palace at the northern end of the fortification. Previously Masada had been partially fortified by the Hasmoneans; on one occasion, prior to gaining control of the Judean throne, Herod himself had escaped there with his family.

More than half a century after Herod's death, in connection with the First Jewish Revolt, Masada received its real test. Jewish zealots seized the fort at the beginning of the revolt in A.D. 66 and continued to hold it after Jerusalem fell to Titus in A.D. 70. The Romans made no attempt to take Masada until A.D. 72. In that year Flavius Silva, the Roman military governor of Jerusalem, began the siege, while Eleazar ben Yair commanded the defending zealots.

Eleazar's Speech to the Rebels at Masada

According to Josephus, Eleazar made the following appeal to his soldiers when it became apparent that they could no longer defend Masada.

My loyal followers, long ago we resolved to serve neither the

Romans nor anyone else but God, who alone is the true and righteous Lord of men: now the time has come to prove our determination by our deeds. We must not disgrace ourselves: hitherto we have refused to submit to slavery, even when it brought no danger with it; we must not choose slavery now. Indeed it will mean the end of everything if we fall alive into the hands of the Romans. For we were the first of all to revolt, and will be the last to break off the struggle. I think it is God who has given us this privilege—the privilege to die nobly and as free men, unlike those who were unexpectedly defeated. It is evident that daybreak will end our resistance, but we are free to choose an honorable death with our loved ones. This our enemies cannot prevent, regardless of how earnestly they pray to take us alive. Nor can we defeat them in battle.

. . . We ought perhaps to have read the mind of God and realized that his once beloved Jewish race had been sentenced to extinction. For if he had remained gracious and only slightly angry with us, he would not have shut his eyes to the destruction of so many thousands or allowed his holy city to be burned to the ground by our enemies. . . .Not even the impregnability of our fortress has saved us. Although we have plenty of goods and weapons, and more than enough other supplies, God himself without a doubt has taken away all hopes of our survival. The fire which was directed toward the enemy lines did not turn back of its own accord toward the wall we had built. These things are God's vengeance for the many wrongs which we in our madness have done to our countrymen. For those wrongs let us pay the penalty to God, by our own hands and not to the Romans. It will be easier to bear. Let our wives die unabused, our children without knowledge of slavery. After that, let us do each other an ungrudging kindness, preserving our freedom as a glorious winding-sheet. But first let our possessions and the whole fortress go up in flames. It will be a bitter blow to the Romans to find that they neither can do harm to us nor loot our possessions. One thing only let us spare—our store of food.

The food supply will bear witness when we are dead to the fact that we perished, not through starvation but because, as we had resolved from the beginning, we chose death rather than slavery.

(*Jewish War*, Book VII, Ch. 8)

The rebels heeded Eleazar's appeal, according to Josephus, and committed mass suicide, and 960 people died in this fashion by Josephus' figures. Only two women and five children survived by hiding in an underground cavern.

Silva constructed a massive earth and stone ramp on the west side of the mountain, allowing the Romans access to a section of the wall. After almost a year of siege the Romans were able to breach the wall and destroy any hopes the zealots had of holding Masada longer. At that point, according to Josephus, Eleazar and his fellow zealots chose suicide instead of Roman swords.

Storehouse
remains
on
Masada

In my opinion Masada ranks with Petra as an absolute "must" for any tour of the Middle East. It is not only the archaeological remains that are so fascinating, but the union of these impressive man-made remains with their awesome natural setting as well. Because Masada can be very hot, especially in the summertime, plan to arrive reasonably early in the morning. The drive from modern Arad takes about 45 minutes; there is a cable car to the top.

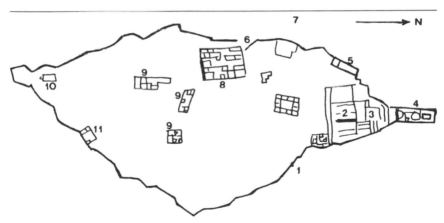

1 Snake Path Gate (Cable Car)	7 Siege Ramp
2 Storerooms	8 Herod's Western Palace
3 Bathhouse	9 Small Palaces
4 Herod's Three-tiered Palace	10 Pool
5 Synagogue	11 Southern (Cistern) Gate
6 Western gate	

MASADA RUINS DETAIL

En Gedi. After a morning exploring Masada, En Gedi is a convenient stop both for lunch and for a swim in the Dead Sea. En Gedi (Ain Gedi in Arabic) means "the spring of the kid." The actual spring is beyond the cliffs which overlook the Dead Sea. Archaeological investigations in the vicinity of the spring indicate settlements from the Chalcolithic period, the time of the Judean monarchy, and the Hellenistic-Roman-Byzantine periods.

According to 1 Samuel 24:1, David once escaped from Saul to "the wilderness of En Gedi." En Gedi is mentioned also in Joshua 15:62, 2 Chronicles 20:2 and Ezekiel 47:10. In Song of Songs 1:14 the poet compares his "beloved" to a "cluster of henna in the vineyards of En Gedi."

The Caves of Nahal Hever and Wady Murabba'at. There are many caves in this rugged Wilderness area. The most famous are the caves at Wady Qumran where the Dead Sea Scrolls were discovered in 1947. In 1951 manuscript fragments were also found in a cave at Wady Murabba'at. Then in 1960-61 the so-called "Cave of Horror" and "Cave of Letters" were discovered on the banks of Nahal Hever. Whereas the Dead Sea Scrolls from Qumran were left by a Jewish religious community of the first century A.D. (the Essenes), the materials from the Murabba'at and Nahal Hever caves were left behind by rebels involved in the Bar Kochba revolt in the second century. Artifacts from all of these caves are on display at the Shrine of the Book of the Israel Museum.

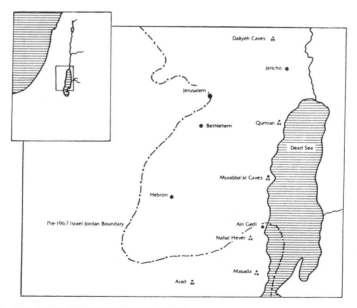

Map 20: DEAD SEA SCROLLS DISCOVERIES

Qumran. The road passes Qumran where the first of the Dead Sea Scrolls were discovered. As indicated above, the Qumran scrolls were left by a Jewish religious community, the Essenes, who occupied the site during the first century A.D. Apparently the Essenes hid their library in the caves only a short time before their community was destroyed by the Romans in connection with the First Jewish Revolt. Qumran is maintained by the Israeli government as a national park and some of the scrolls are on display at the Shrine of the Book of the Israel Museum.

The Scrolls are of two varieties: (1) scrolls of the various books of the Old Testament; (2) other written documents relevant to the Essenes' community organization and worship. They are useful to biblical scholars for two corresponding reasons: (1) The scrolls of the Old Testament books are the oldest biblical manuscripts which have survived; (2) the other written documents provide excellent data concerning the beliefs and activities of a sectarian Jewish community during New Testament times.

Chronology of Dead Sea Scrolls Discoveries

1947	Mohammad ed-Dib's initial discovery of scrolls at Qumran
1948-1949	Qumran Cave I identified by archaeologists and cleared
1951	Further discoveries by Bedouins at Murabba'at Caves
1952-1956	Ten more caves discovered at Qumran by archaeologists; Excavations at Khirbet Qumran
1953	Brief survey of Israeli sector of Dead Sea area (En Gedi to Masada) by Y. Aharoni
1955	Mar Yeshue Samuel's scrolls purchased by the State of Israel ($250,000)
1960-1961	More thorough exploration of Israeli sector: discoveries at Nahal Hever ("Cave of Horror" and "Cave of Letters")
1961-1964	Construction of the "Shrine of the Book"
1962-1964	Discovery and clearance of Daliyeh Caves
1963-1965	Excavations at Masada
1967	Yigael Yadin acquires the "Temple Scroll"

**The Northern Hill Country,
Mediterranean Coast, and Galilee** _____

I suggest a minimum three-day excursion into Galilee, with overnight stops in the Haifa-Acre vicinity on the Mediterranean Sea and at Tiberias on the Sea of Galilee. The itinerary below begins with a full day's drive through the hill country north of Jerusalem to Nablus (ancient Shechem), then northwest to Caesarea on the Mediterranean Coast, and again north across Mount Carmel to Acre. After an early morning visit to the Crusader castle at Acre and Ras en-Nakurah (the Ladder of Tyre), ample time will be available to drive across northern Galilee and to explore the area around the Sea of Galilee. Return to Jerusalem on the third day via southern Galilee, the Jezreel Valley, and the Jordan Valley. The following are some of the highlights to see along the way.

The hill country north of Jerusalem. The tribes of Benjamin, Ephraim and Manasseh occupied this area in Old Testament times. After Solomon's death, when his realm was divided into two lesser kingdoms (Israel in the north and Judah in the south), this area was the core of the northern kingdom (Israel) with Samaria as its capital (1 Kings 12:1-16; 16:23-24). Gradually the entire northern portion of the central hill country came to be known as "the mountain of Samaria" (Amos 4:1), or simply "Samaria" (John 4:4). Israel was conquered and its cities destroyed by the Assyrians in 722 B.C., but survivors of this Old Testament kingdom still lived in the northern hill country in New Testament times. These were the Samaritans of Jesus' day.

Many of the villages one reads about in the Old Testament narratives were clustered in the hill country within a range of twelve or fifteen miles north of Jerusalem. Some of the names of these old villages are preserved in those of contemporary Arab towns nestled in these same hills. Rather than actually visiting the towns, I suggest climbing one of the prominent hills for a panoramic view: Tell el-Ful is easily accessible from the main Jerusalem-Nablus road; Nebi Samwil provides a fascinating view; a favorite of mine is the hill between Beitin and et-Tell (ancient Bethel and Ai), undoubtedly the place referred to in Genesis 12:8 and 13:14-17.

Seilun. Site of ancient Shiloh (Joshua 18:21-22; Judges 21; 1 Samuel 1-4; Jeremiah 7:12-14; 26:6-9; Psalms 78:60). This village, approximately halfway between Jerusalem and Nablus and also near the main Jerusalem-Nablus road, appears as Shillo on modern Israeli maps. Just north of Seilun/Shillo the road makes a steep descent into the valley of Lubban, or ancient Lebonah (see Judges 21:19).

Map 21: NORTHERN HILL COUNTRY, MEDITERRANEAN
COAST, AND GALILEE

Villages North of Jerusalem

The Arab names of the little villages immediately north of Jerusalem (compare Map 22) are reminiscent of the biblical names of villages which are known to have existed in that vicinity. This is a result, no doubt, of old Semitic names surviving the Hellenistic-Roman-Byzantine periods and reemerging during the Arabic period.

Arabic name	Biblical name	Arabic name	Biblical name
Beitin	Bethel (See Genesis 12:8; 1 Kings 12:29; Amos 7:10)		Judges 20:10ff.; 1 Samuel 13:3ff.; 1 Kings 15:22)
Rammun	Rimmon (Judges 20:45-47; Zechariah 14:10)	er-Ram	Ramah (1 Samuel 1:19; Isaiah 10:29; Jeremiah 31:15; 40:1; Hosea 5:8)
el-Bira	Beeroth (Joshua 9:17, 2 Samuel 4:2; Ezra 2:25)	el-Jib	Gibeon (Joshua 9:3ff.; 2 Samuel 2:12ff.; 1 Kings 3:4ff.)
Mukhmas	Michmash (1 Samuel 13:5ff.; Nehemiah 11:31; Isaiah 10:28)	Anata	Anathoth (Joshua 21:18; 1 Kings 2:26; Jeremiah 1:1; 11:21ff.)
Jaba	Geba (also spelled Gibeah.		

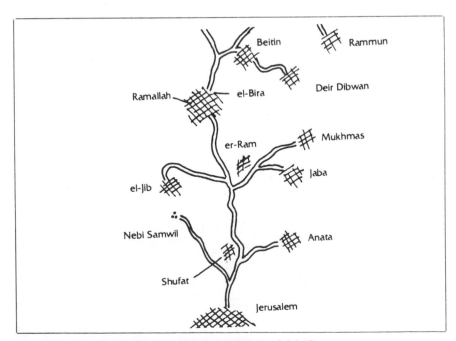

Map 22: VILLAGES ALONG THE JERUSALEM-NABLUS ROAD

Tell Balata (Shechem). Shechem, at the eastern entrance to the pass between Mount's Ebal and Gerizim, was ancient before the Israelites appeared in the Holy Land and was significant throughout the Old Testament period (see Map 7 and notes, above). The ruins of ancient Shechem, called Tell Balata, are within the city limits of modern Nablus. Excavations of these ruins confirm that Shechem was an active city during the Bronze and Iron Ages, but uninhabited during the fifth and fourth centuries B.C., and then revived near the end of the fourth century. Scholars speculate that the new settlers at the end of the fourth century were refugees from Samaria, which was destroyed in circumstances relating to a revolt against Alexander the Great (see below). Shechem became an important Samaritan center during the Hellenistic period, and the Samaritans built a sanctuary on Mount Gerizim. Both the city and the sanctuary were destroyed in 129 B.C. by John Hyrcanus, one of the Hasmonean (Jewish) kings of Jerusalem.

Jacob's Well. A century later, when Jesus encountered a Samaritan woman at Jacob's well, antagonism between Samaritans and Jews remained intense. Jesus' conversation with the woman is described in John 4. The mountain to which she referred must have been Gerizim, indicating that the village of Sychar and the well must have been in the same immediate vicinity. What is today considered Jacob's well was marked with a church as early as the fourth century A.D. The partially completed church there today was begun at the turn of the century. Work on it ceased in 1914.

Nablus (Neapolis). In A.D. 72 Titus founded a new city at the western entrance to the pass between Ebal and Gerizim. He named it Flavia Neapolis ("Flavia" in honor of Flavius Vespasian; "Neapolis" means "the new city").

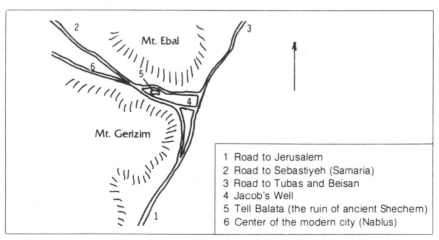

NABLUS AND VICINITY

Nablus is the Arabic form of Neapolis. The first settlers of Neapolis were Roman Legionaries. Later, after this "new city" was approximately a century old, the Emperor Hadrian constructed a temple to Jupiter on Mount Gerizim, which towered above. Modern Nablus is one of the major cities in the Holy Land; it continues to grow and includes within its limits both Tell Balata and the traditional site of Jacob's well.

Sebastiyeh (Samaria). Omri selected this site as capital of the northern Israelite kingdom. Ahab and Jezebel ruled here, and archaeologists have found the remains of an impressive palace on the acropolis, generally attributed to Ahab.

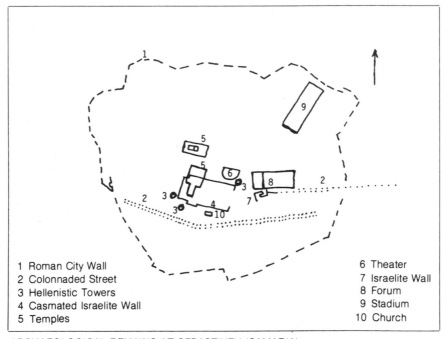

1 Roman City Wall
2 Colonnaded Street
3 Hellenistic Towers
4 Casmated Israelite Wall
5 Temples

6 Theater
7 Israelite Wall
8 Forum
9 Stadium
10 Church

ARCHAEOLOGICAL REMAINS AT SEBASTIYEH (SAMARIA)

Key Moments in the History of Samaria-Sebastiyeh

• Site selected by Omri in the ninth century B.C. for a new capital city of the northern Israelite kingdom (1 Kings 16:23-24). Omri named the new city Samaria, after the man from whom he purchased the land.

- Ahab and Jezebel rule from Samaria; the city figures prominently in biblical narratives about Elijah and Elisha (1 Kings 17-2 Kings 10) and in the pronouncements of the Latter Prophets (Amos 4:1; 8:14; Hosea 7:1; 10:7; Isaiah 7:9).
- The northern kingdom, including its capital city Samaria, falls to the Assyrians in 722 B.C. The entire northern hill country becomes an Assyrian province.
- Samaria still continues as a city under Persian rule. One of the Persian-appointed governors of Samaria, Sanballat, opposes Nehemiah's attempt to revive Jerusalem (Nehemiah 2:19; 4:17).
- Alexander the Great crushes a Samaritan revolt and settles 6,000 Greeks from Macedonia in the city. Samaritan refugees resettle in Shechem and build a temple on Mount Gerizim.
- John Hyrcanus, one of the Hasmonean rulers of Jerusalem, destroys Samaria, Shechem, and the Samaritan temple on Mount Gerizim.
- Pompey reestablishes Samaria in 64 B.C.
- Caesar Augustus grants Samaria to Herod in 30 B.C. Herod renames the city Sebastos (the Greek equivalent of "Augustus") and undertakes a massive building program (a temple on the acropolis dedicated to Augustus, a theater, a stadium, a colonnaded street and other structures).
- Sebastos becomes an important Christian center during the Byzantine period, boasting several churches and a monastery. According to Christian tradition which circulated at that time, John the Baptist was buried at Sebastos.

Samaria became a thoroughly Greek city following Alexander the Great's conquest and huge stone towers still standing at the site represent city fortifications from the Hellenistic period. But most of the architectural remains seen at the site today date from the reign of Herod the Great. Caesar Augustus gave Samaria to Herod in 30 B.C. Accordingly, Herod renamed the city Sebastos (Greek for Augustus), as preserved in the modern Arab name Sebastiyeh. Among the structures Herod built at Sebastos, including a theater, stadium, and colonnaded street, was a temple on the acropolis which he dedicated to Caesar.

According to early Christian tradition, John the Baptist was buried at Sebastos.

Caesarea. Originally called Straton's Tower, this seaport is mentioned in written records as early as the middle of the third century B.C. It was governed by various rulers, including Cleopatra, before Caesar Augustus turned it over to Herod the Great. Herod built an enclosed deep sea harbor, surrounded the city with a wall and renamed it Caesarea. More important for the future of the city, he constructed an aqueduct to bring fresh water from springs in Mount Carmel. Caesarea became the chief Roman administrative center of Judea in A.D. 6—this official status explains why Paul was imprisoned there before being sent to Rome (Acts 23:23-26:33. See also Acts 9:30; 10:1, 24; 11:11; 12:19-23; 21:8). The population of Caesarea was mixed, Gentile and Jewish, resulting in numerous disputes, including a clash in A.D. 66 that sparked the first Jewish Revolt.

Caesarea aqueduct

Caesarea was already an important center of Christian learning in the third century A.D., even before Christianity was legalized. Origen taught there, for example. One of his students, Eusebius, wrote a history of the early church and played a leading role at the Council of Nicea. Caesarea's greatest expansion took place during the Byzantine period. The last city in the Holy Land to fall to the Arabs, Caesarea was defeated in A.D. 640.

When the Crusaders conquered Caesarea in 1101, they discovered what they believed to be the Holy Grail, the "Sacro Catino," today preserved in the Cathedral of San Lorenzo, Genoa. Saladin destroyed the Crusader fortifications at Caesarea in 1187, but in 1191 the Crusaders recovered Caesarea and it remained a key Crusader stronghold for the next half century . The fortifications evident at Caesarea today were built by Louis IX in 1251-52. Finally in 1265, Caesarea fell to Baybars, the famous Mamluk ruler, who systematically destroyed the city and left it in ruins. These ruins served as a quarry for nearby villages throughout the Mamluk and Ottoman periods.

Several archaeological teams have already excavated at Caesarea and work continues. Due to the city's size, however, especially in Byzantine times, archaeologists have barely scratched the surface. Among the archaeological finds made here is an inscription referring to Pontius Pilate and a fragment of another which refers to Nazareth.

Reference to Pontius Pilate in an Inscription from Caesarea

A team of Italian archaeologists excavating the Roman theater at Caesarea in 1961 discovered an inscription which refers to Pontius Pilate. Probably this was a dedicatory inscription originally embedded in the wall of a building erected during Pilate's term of office. The stone on which the inscription appears was later reused in the construction of the theater, however, at which time the inscription was damaged. It probably read as follows:

[CAESARIEN] S [IBUS]	To the people of Caesarea
TIBERIEUM	Tiberieum
PON]TIUSPILATUS	Pon tius Pilate
PRAEF]ECTUSIUDA[EA]E	Pref ect of Judea

Mount Carmel/Mount Carmel Caves. Mount Carmel, a spur of the central hill country, juts into the Mediterranean Sea at Haifa and is perhaps best remembered as the place Elijah confronted the prophets of Baal (1 Kings 18). On the western slopes of Mount Carmel, midway between Caesarea and Haifa, are three caves where Paleolithic human and artifactual remains have been discovered. The excavations were conducted during the early 1930s and revealed skeletal remains with Neanderthal characteristics, popularly known as "Mount Carmel Man."

Haifa. A major port city has emerged here only in modern times, beginning in the mandate period. The city has now spread to the top of Mount Carmel, from which a panoramic view of the harbor and the Jezreel Valley is possible.

View of harbor at Haifa.

Acre (Acco). Mentioned in Bronze Age Egyptian texts, Acco rose to prominence as a seaport and commercial center in the Hellenistic Period. Ptolemy II had the city rebuilt at that time and renamed it Ptolemais. It is called Ptolemais in Acts 21:7, in connection with one of Paul's journeys. Acco was also a prominent Crusader city called St. Jean d'Acre, or simply Acre. Acre fell to Saladin after the crucial battle of the Horns of Hattin in 1187. But Crusaders recovered it in 1191 and it served as their main base in the Holy Land for another hundred years. Finally, in 1291, after a forty-three-day siege, Acre fell to the Mamluks. The city's inhabitants (30,000 or more) who could not escape to ships waiting offshore were slain or sold as slaves. This ended Crusader presence in the Holy Land.

Acre's commercial growth in the Crusader period was spurred by merchants from Genoa, Venice, Pisa, and Amalfi. Military and governmental power lay in the hands of various orders of knights, including the Knights Templars, the Teutonic Knights, the Order of St. Lazarus, and the Hospitallers (the Order of the Knights of St. John). The Hospitallers were the strongest order and erected an enormous military and government citadel in the center of the city. A part of this Hospitallers' section of Crusader Acre recently has been excavated and opened to the public.

Acre reemerged both politically and militarily in the mid-eighteenth century, playing an important role in Middle Eastern history for the next hundred years.

Acre under Turkish Rule

The Holy Land was part of the vast Ottoman empire from the sixteenth century to World War I. For administrative purposes, the Ottoman empire was divided into "pashaliks," each governed by a "pasha" answerable to the "Porte" in Istanbul. The Ottoman empire had reached an advanced state of decline by the mid-eighteenth century, however, to the extent that the pashas and local sheikhs often exerted independent power. Three colorful political leaders from the period whose careers involved Acre were Daher el-Omar, Ahmed al-Jazzar and Mohammad Ali.

Daher el-Omar (1749-1775)—Sheikh of a Bedouin tribe settled in Galilee, Daher seized Acre in 1749, improved the defenses of the city, and ruled Galilee wisely for the next quarter of a century. He was supported by Ali Bey, a Mamluk ruler of Egypt who had thoughts of conquering Syria. Daher even secured the aid of the Russian navy during the Russo-Turkish War. Ali Bey died in 1773; Russia made peace with the Ottoman government in 1774; Daher was defeated and killed by an Ottoman army (led by the Pasha of Damascus) in 1775.

Ahmed al-Jazzar (1775-1804)—This Mamluk slave (actually Bosnian by birth) established a military reputation in Syria and was appointed by the Ottoman government to succeed Daher el-Omar at Acre. As it turned out, al-Jazzar also carved out an essentially independent kingdom which included much of Syria and Palestine. Al-Jazzar defended Acre successfully against Napoleon in 1799, with the aid of a British squadron under Sir Sidney Smith, and continued to rule until his death in 1804. His cruel and self-serving governmental policies are reflected in his nickname, "al-Jazzar" ("the Butcher").

Mohammad Ali (1832-1839)—Among the soldiers who defended Acre against Napoleon in 1799 was this Albanian army officer. In 1808 he was appointed Pasha of Egypt. Three years later he put a final end to the long-standing Mamluk influence in Egypt by entrapping and massacring all of the Mamluk lords on a single occasion. With a power base thus firmly established in Egypt, Mohammad Ali turned his attention to Syria-Palestine, where he and his son (Ibrahim) exerted a dominating influence for the next two decades. For nine years of this time Mohammad Ali enjoyed direct control of Syria-Palestine—that is, from 1831 when Ibrahim invaded the Holy Land and conquered Acre (the city actually fell in May, 1832), to 1839 when the European powers intervened and restored Syria-Palestine to the Ottoman Sultan.

Ras en-Nakurah (The Ladder of Tyre). Acre is located on a coastal plain interrupted on the north and south by mountain spurs which jut into the Mediterranean Sea. The mountain spur to the south is Mount Carmel; the one to the north is Ras en-Nakurah (Rosh Hanikra in Hebrew). Ras en-Nakurah is often called the Ladder of Tyre, since the ancient city of Tyre is not far beyond. Both Mount Carmel and Ras en-Nakurah provide magnificent views of the Mediterranean coastline.

Safed/Meron/Khirbet Shema. After the disaster of the Jewish revolts of A.D. 66-70 and 132-135, the center of Jewish religious leadership shifted to Galilee. One of the centers of Talmudic scholarship which emerged in Galilee was Safed, a city perched high on a hill overlooking the Sea of Galilee. During the Middle Ages Safed became a center of a mystical Jewish movement known as Kabalism. The Jewish population at Safed was virtually replaced by Christian and then by Muslim populations during the Crusader and post-Crusader periods; before 1948 the entire area was still mainly Arab. But a small Jewish community persisted at Safed through the centuries, and today it is a predominantly Jewish city.

Remains of a third century synagogue can be seen on an opposite hill at Meron. A "mikveh," or ritual bath, approximately the same age as the Meron synagogue, has been uncovered by archaeologists at nearby Khirbet Shema.

Tell el-Qedah (Hazor). Tell el-Qedah is the remains of ancient Hazor, certainly one of the largest and most impressive cities in the entire eastern Mediterranean Seaboard during the Bronze Age. Hazor had dwindled to a much smaller settlement before the Israelite settlement of Canaan (Joshua 11:10; Judges 4:2). It was refortified by Solomon (1 Kings 9:15) and was later expanded somewhat, apparently by Ahab. Full-scale excavations at the site in the fifties revealed twenty-one occupational phases ranging from Early Bronze Age to Hellenistic. Hazor is today maintained as a national park, with Iron Age (Israelite) levels uncovered and displayed. The water system, probably dating from Ahab's reign, is especially interesting.

Tell el-Qadi (Dan) and Banyas (Caesarea Philippi). The Jordan River originates from springs at the foot of Mount Hermon and eventually flows into the Dead Sea. Dan and Panias were ancient sanctuaries associated with two of these springs. Dan is remembered in the Old Testament as one of the places (the other was Bethel) where Jeroboam I erected a golden calf (see 1 Kings 12:26-33; also Judges 17-18). Panias may be identical with Baal-Gad of the Old Testament (Joshua 11:17; 12:7; 13:5). In any case, this spot was sacred to the god Pan in Hellenistic times, which explains why it was called Panias. Banyas is Arabic for Panias.

Caesar Augustus added Panias to Herod the Great's kingdom in 20 B.C.; Herod, in turn, constructed a temple there dedicated to Augustus. When Herod died and the kingdom was divided among his three surviving sons, the area northeast of the Sea of Galilee, including Panias, fell to Herod Philip. Herod Philip selected Panias as his capital, undertook an extensive building program there, and renamed the place Caesarea. This Caesarea is usually termed Caesarea Philippi (Matthew 16:13; Mark 8:27) to distinguish it from the other Caesarea on the Mediterranean Coast.

Tell Hum (Capernaum). It is almost definite that Tell Hum, lying on the northern shore of the Sea of Galilee, is the site of ancient Capernaum. Capernaum and its synagogue pervades the gospels' account of Jesus' ministry (Matthew 4:13; 11:23; Mark 1:21; Luke 7:1; 10:15; John 6:59). Several of the disciples, including Peter, seem to have been fishermen from Capernaum; Matthew 4:13 indicates that Jesus lived there for a time. The partially preserved synagogue at Tell Hum / Capernaum postdates the one which Jesus and his disciples knew. Probably the one observable today is from the third century A.D.

According to Egeria, a nun from one of the western provinces of the Roman empire who visited the Holy Land between 381 and 384, Peter's house still stood at that late date and had been converted into a church: "In Capernaum out of the house of the first of the apostles a church was made, the walls of which stand until today as they once were. Here the Lord cured the paralytic." Archaeologists have excavated what may be the remains of this fourth century church. It lies between the synagogue and sea, its structure octagon, and it clearly dates from the Byzantine period. Whether Egeria's information was correct about this marking the actual site of Peter's house is another question.

Mount of Beatitudes. Matthew 5-7 records Jesus' Sermon on the Mount, which begins with the beatitudes. No specific geographical information is provided; we are told simply that "seeing the crowds, he went up on the mountain. . . ." There is no way of knowing where this mountain was located, therefore, except that it must have been somewhere near the Sea of Galilee. The Gospel of Luke does not even indicate that these teachings were given on a mountain. While the traditional "Mount of Beatitudes," which overlooks the Sea of Galilee from the northwest, has no pretext to authenticity, it is a beautiful spot and well worth a visit.

Tabgha. Neither is there any evidence to support the tradition that Tabgha, on the shore of the Sea of Galilee immediately west of Capernaum and at the foot of the traditional Mount of Beatitudes, is where Jesus fed the five thousand. Note that Matthew 14:13-34 places this event on an opposite shore of the Sea of Galilee from Gennesaret (see also Matthew 15:32-38; Mark 6:32-44; Luke 9:10-17; John 6:1-13).

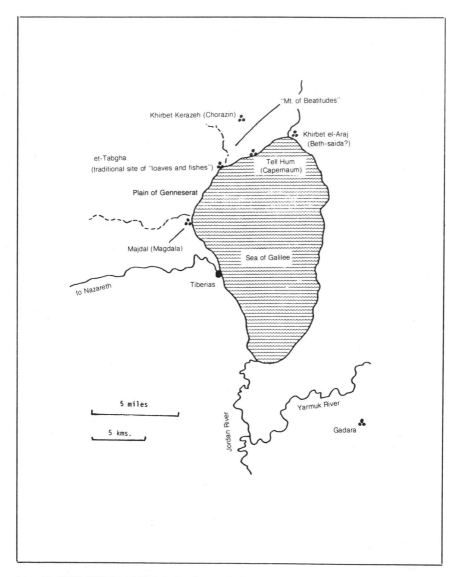

Map 23: NEW TESTAMENT SITES NEAR THE SEA OF GALILEE

Chorazin. The ruins of Khirbet Kerazeh, northwest of the Sea of Galilee, represent ancient Chorazin, perhaps best remembered for Jesus' pronouncement:

> Woe to you, Chorazin! Woe to you, Beth-saida! for if
> the mighty works done in you had been done in Tyre
> and Sidon, they would have repented long ago in
> sackcloth and ashes.

Among the ruins at Khirbet Kerazeh are the remains of a third century synagogue. The location of ancient Beth-saida is uncertain. Khirbet el-Araj, near the point where the Jordan enters the Sea of Galilee, is a possibility. (See Matthew 11:21; Mark 6:45; 8:22; Luke 9:10; 10:13; John 1:44 and 12:21).

Gennesaret. This pleasant, fertile plain on the northwestern shore of the Sea of Galilee is described at length by Josephus, who even refers to the Sea of Galilee as the "Sea of Gennesar." Matthew 14:34 and Mark 6:53 record that Jesus and the disciples crossed the sea to the land of Gennesaret, or Gennesar, after feeding the five thousand.

Magdala. At the southern end of the Plain of Gennesaret is the site of ancient Magdala. This old name is preserved in the Arabic name, Majdal. On modern Israeli maps it appears as Magdal. Mary Magdalene was from Magdala, her name meaning "Mary of Magdala."

Tiberias. Herod Antipas founded this city in A.D. 20, calling it Tiberias after the Roman emperor of the same name. Soon it replaced Sepphoris as capital of northern Galilee. Initially, few Jews settled in Tiberias because it was established on the site of a cemetery. But following the Bar Kochba revolt in the second century A.D., Tiberias became an important center for Jewish learning. Rabbi Judah ha-Nasi, compiler of the Mishnah, was a resident during the early third century. The Palestinian Talmud was largely the work of Jewish interpreters active at Tiberias near the end of the fourth century. Two centuries later, Jewish scholars there designed a system of vowel points for the Hebrew text of the Old Testament. They also developed a "Massorah," an extensive set of notes intended to guard the biblical text against copying errors which sometimes occurred during the transmitting process from one generation to the next.

Still an important city, Tiberias fell in 1099 to Tancred, the famous Crusader leader. Later it belonged to the fiefdom of Guy de Lusignan; and in 1187, responding to Lusignan's call for help in the face of a Muslim attack, Crusaders from throughout the Holy Land mustered for war and marched toward Tiberias. This combined Crusader army was out-maneuvered and crushed by Saladin at the Horns of Hattin (see below).

Tiberias was left a desolate ruin at the end of the Crusader period, the Jews of the city having fled when the Crusaders first arrived in 1099, and the Crusader population having been massacred by the Mamluks in 1247. The site remained virtually unoccupied until the eighteenth century when Daher el-Omar (see above, under "Acre under Turkish Rule") rebuilt the city walls and sponsored resettlement. The new settlers were primarily Jewish, led by Rabbi Hayyim Abulafia from Turkey.

Maimonides, the famous Talmudic scholar and courtier of Saladin, is buried in Tiberias. Maimonides' full name and title was Rabbi Moshe Ben Maimon, sometimes abbreviated "Rambam." He died in Cairo in 1204 while the Palestinian coast was still in Crusader hands. Apparently Maimonides' students brought his body to the Holy Land for burial. According to legend, they followed the camel bearing the coffin toward Tiberias until the camel kneeled just outside the walls of the city. There they buried their master, and the tomb is revered by Jews even today.

Horns of Hattin. The road from Tiberias to Nazareth passes a conspicuous, elongated hill, taller at its ends. Resembling a saddle, the humps at the ends serve as saddle horns. On July 4, 1187 these "Horns of Hattin" witnessed the massacre of the combined armies of the Crusader kingdom of Jerusalem at the hands of Saladin. With the battle obviously lost, a small desperate band of knights made a last stand on the hill itself. Later in the day, Saladin set up his pavilion on the hill and received the defeated nobles. Raynold de Chatillon, the treacherous lord of Kerak who had angered Saladin by attacking Muslim pilgrims on their way to Mecca was beheaded. (See "Kerak," above, under "The 'King's Highway' to Petra and Aqaba.")

For all practical purposes the year 1187 ended the Crusader kingdom in the Holy Land. All but a few of the fighting men were slain or taken prisoner at Hattin. Within the year one after another of the Crusader castles fell to Saladin. A Crusader presence lingered in the Holy Land for another century, and later Crusades were organized in hopes of recovering the lost kingdom. But none of these later Crusades were very successful.

Kefr Cana. Although the location of Cana of Galilee, the place where Jesus attended the wedding feast (John 2:1; 21:2), is unknown, Kafar Kanna between Tiberias and Nazareth is a reasonable candidate. Supported by tradition, Kafar Kanna is sometimes designated Cana on modern maps. Another possibility, whose Arabic name seems more likely to have derived from the biblical name Cana, is Qana el-Jelil. It is located approximately nine miles north of Nazareth.

Nazareth. When Jesus was a boy, Nazareth was only three or four miles from Sepphorus, the Roman administrative capital of Galilee. Nazareth itself, however, has always been only a small village until recently. In fact, the New Testatment and an inscription fragment discovered at Caesarea in 1962 are the only ancient sources which even mention Nazareth, and the New Testament implies that it was regarded as a rather insignificant place (John 1:46).

Except for the village spring, none of the places in Nazareth associated by tradition with events in the life of Mary, Joseph and Jesus can be verified. Everyone in Nazareth, including the Holy Family, would certainly have used the spring. Two of the churches at Nazareth deserve special mention: the Church of Saint Gabriel, marking the source of the spring, and the magnificent new Church of the Annunciation. The Church of the Annunciation was begun in 1955, replacing an earlier structure built in 1730 and enlarged in 1877. Excavations have revealed that an even older (Byzantine) church once stood on the site.

Jezreel/Mount Tabor. Nazareth is nestled in the hills of southern Galilee, overlooking the Jezreel/Esdraelon Valley. The road from Nazareth across the Jezreel to Megiddo passes near Mount Tabor (see scripture passages cited with Map 6, above), Endor, where a medium called forth Samuel from the dead to speak with Saul (1 Samuel 28:7-14), and Nain, where Jesus raised a widow's son from death (Luke 7:11-15). Tradition identifies Mount Tabor as the mountain of the Transfiguration (Luke 9:28-36). Nain may be identical with Old Testament Shunem where Elisha is also reported to have raised a child from death (2 Kings 4).

Tell el-Mutesellim (Megiddo). Megiddo was one of the most famous and strategically located cities of Bronze-Iron Age Palestine. It commands the Arah Pass, connecting the Jezreel Valley with the coastal plain to the southwest. The main road to Egypt (Way of the Sea; see Map 5, above) led through this pass.

Numerous battles have been fought at Megiddo. The earliest recorded conflict was between Thutmose III and a coalition of Syro-Palestinian kings in the fifteenth century B.C.. Eight hundred years later Josiah would meet his death at Megiddo in a struggle with Pharaoh Neco (2 Kings 23:28-30). Josiah was considered a good and faithful king; his untimely death at Megiddo raised some serious theological questions for the ancient Jews: Why had God allowed Neco to triumph? Why had evil overcome good? Eventually Megiddo became the symbol of a great battle anticipated for the future, when good would finally triumph.

Megiddo was situated on a hill near the entrance to the Arah pass. The word for "hill" or "mountain" in Hebrew is "har." Thus Megiddo could be

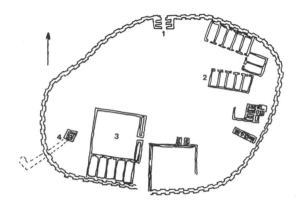

1 Gate
2 North "Stable" Complex
3 South "Stable" Complex
4 Water System

MEGIDDO (OMRIDE PERIOD)

spoken of as "har-megiddo," or Mount Megiddo. The Greek form of "har-megiddo" is "Armageddon" (see Revelation 16:16).

The tell of ancient Megiddo, Tell el-Mutesellim, was extensively excavated by the University of Chicago in 1925-39. Additional soundings were made by Y. Yadin in 1960 and after. Today the site is preserved as a national park. Interesting aspects include the "high place" from the Early Bronze Age, portions of a Solomonic city gate, and an impressive water system, probably dating from the time of Ahab and Jezebel.

Beth Shean. The road from Megiddo to Beth Shean, cutting through the eastern end of the Jezreel Valley, passes near the site of the ancient village of Jezreel where Naboth and Jezebel met their deaths (1 Kings 21: 2 Kings 9-10). Also along this road are Bet Alfa, famous for its sixth century mosaic, and Mount Gilboa, where Saul and Jonathan were slain (1 Samuel 31). Their bodies were carried to Beth Shean, a city which dominated the eastern end of the Jezreel Valley. Beth Shean must have had close relations with Egypt during the latter's empire age; inscriptions from the reigns of Seti I, late fourteenth century B.C., and Rameses II, early thirteenth century, have been discovered there.

Beth Shean was renamed Scythopolis, or "city of the Scythians," in the Hellenistic period. Scythian mercenaries are known to have been in the service of Ptolemy II (285-246 B.C.). Perhaps a colony of Scythian mercenaries settled at Beth Shean. A well-preserved Roman theater at Beth Shean dates from the latter part of the second century A.D. and seats 4500-5000 spectators.

Jericho. Return to Jerusalem through the Jordan Valley. The northern part of the valley is well watered and a luscious green, but proceeding southward it becomes increasingly dry and barren. At the southern end, where the Jordan River enters the Dead Sea, a virtual wasteland exists. On the west side of the Jordan, near its entrance into the Dead Sea, is a major spring; the famous oasis of Jericho. Excavations at Tell es-Sultan, the ruins of ancient Jericho adjacent to the spring, revealed a Neolithic settlement datable to approximately 7000 B.C. This Neolithic Jericho is one of the earliest known villages; the still visible Neolithic tower is, correspondingly, one of the earliest known man-made fortifications.

Jericho flourished during the Early and Middle Bronze Ages, but archaeologists have not been able to establish that a city of any size stood on the site during the Late Bronze and Iron Ages. This is somewhat surprising, since most biblical scholars would date the Israelite conquest of Canaan in the Late Bronze Age (1500-1200 B.C.). The biblical account of the conquest clearly implies that Jericho was a major fortified city at the time (see especially Joshua 1-6). Jericho is mentioned several other times in the Old Testament (see 2 Samuel 10:5; 1 Kings 16:34; 2 Kings 2:4; 18-22. See also Judges 3:13 and 2 Chronicles 28:15, where Jericho is called the "city of palm-trees.").

Eventually the old tell was abandoned, and during the Hellenistic-Roman period a new settlement emerged a short distance to the west. This was the Jericho of New Testament times. Herod the Great erected several imposing structures in Jericho and it was here that he died. Later, in A.D. 724, the Umayyad caliph Hisham built a luxurious winter palace north of the spring.

Part Three

For Further Reference

History of the Holy Land in Outline

In Part I of this guide book we divided the whole long sweep of archaeological and historical time in the Middle East into eleven periods—one extremely long period designated "Prehistoric Times" plus ten historical periods. Archaeologists subdivide Prehistoric Times as follows:

Paleolithic (Old Stone) Period

From the earliest evidences of human occupation (at least as early as 300,000 years ago in the Holy Land and probably much earlier) to roughly the end of the last glacial phase (ca. 10,000 B.C.). Fossils and tools from the Mount Carmel caves date from the Paleolithic Period.

Mesolithic (Middle Stone) Period

From ca. 10,000 to ca. 7000 B.C.—that is, from the end of the last glacial phase to the first appearance of farming villages in the Middle East. This was a transitional period during which the beginnings of agriculture and domestication of animals probably occurred.

Neolithic (New Stone) Period

From ca. 7000 to 4000 B.C. The earliest villages (Jericho for example) emerged during this period. The technique for firing pottery was developed ca. 5500 B.C.

Chalcolithic (Copper-Stone) Period

From ca. 4000 to 3200 B.C. This was another transitional period during which numerous localized cultures existed in the Holy Land and urban centers began to emerge in the Tigris-Euphrates

Valley. Ivory and copper artifacts from the vicinity of En Gedi and Beersheba on display in the Israel Museum represent the excellent craftsmenship of the period.

Each of the ten historical periods has its own story to be told, and we will deal with them, each in turn, below. As we also noted in Part I of the guidebook, however, it is useful to lump these ten periods into four major historical phases. Geographical terms and place names have changed from time to time in the Holy Land, and these changes tend to have occurred in accordance with the four phases.

Bronze-Iron Ages (ca. 3200-333 B.C.)

This was the time of the most ancient kingdoms and empires— Egypt, Babylon, Assyria, Persia, Edom, Moab, Israel and others. Semitic languages and Semitic place names predominated in the Fertile Crescent, including the Holy Land. Ancient fortified cities emerged, flourished and produced stratified "tells." Among the famous ancient cities in the Holy Land which produced tells were Hazor, Megiddo, Jericho and Arad.

Hellenistic-Roman-Byzantine Periods (333 B.C.-A.D. 640)

For a thousand years the Mediterranean world, including the eastern Mediterranean seaboard of which the Holy Land is a part, was dominated by Greek- and Latin-speaking peoples. Greek- and Latin-based names replaced the old Semitic names. Classical Greek and Roman style cities in the Holy Land were Sebastos (Samaria), Gerasa (Jerash), Caesarea and Petra. The Herodium and Masada were strategic fortifications.

Early Arab-Crusader-Mamluk-Ottoman Periods (A.D. 640-1918)

Under Arab influence Semitic names predominated once again. Many of the old names from the Bronze-Iron Ages reemerged with slightly different pronunciations. Typical archaeological remains are Islamic monuments and mosques (Dome of the Rock and al-Aksa in Jerusalem) and Crusader castles (Acre, Caesarea, Kerak). The walls which surrounded the old city of Jerusalem date from early Ottoman times.

Mandate Period and following (1918-   )

The Middle East today is very much a part of the modern world— concrete, steel, traffic jams and all. Semitic names continue to predominate. There has been a tendency in Israel to revive biblical names and to replace Arabic names with Hebrew equivalents.

While lumping the ten historical periods into four major phases helps one get a better grasp of the overall picture, each of these ten periods represents a significant block of time and deserves individual attention. Let us look at them now each in turn. Compare also the chronological charts below.

Bronze Age: The Most Ancient Kingdoms and Empires. The Bronze Age represents the first two millennia of recorded history in the Middle East. Most of the records available from this early period are from Mesopotamia, Anatolia and Egypt, however, and provide very little direct information about people and events in the Holy Land. Biblical historians usually date the Hebrew patriarchs (Abraham, Isaac and Jacob) in the Bronze Age and date the exodus from Egypt under Moses at the very end of this age. Archaeologists subdivide the Bronze Age as follows:

§ *Early Bronze Age.* ca. 3200-2200 B.C. City-states flourished throughout the Fertile Crescent—Sumerian cities in southern Mesopotamia, for example, and the recently discovered city of Ebla in Syria. This period witnessed the conquests of Sargon of Akkad and the building of the pyramids. Near the end of the period (Early Bronze IV, ca. 2300-2200) many of the city-states in the Holy Land met with destruction followed by largely nomadic or semi-nomadic occupation. Egypt experienced her "First Intermediate Period" about the same time.

§ *Middle Bronze Age.* ca. 2200-1550 B.C. The first part of this age (Middle Bronze I, ca. 2200-2000, and Middle Bronze II, ca. 2000-1800) witnessed the establishment of Amorite dynasties in many of the Mesopotamian cities (Isin, Larsa, Mari, Babylon and others) and corresponded roughly to the "Middle Kingdom Period" in Egypt's history. Gradually the city-states began to flourish again in the Holy Land as well. The latter part of the Middle Bronze Age (Middle Bronze II B, ca. 1800-1650, and Middle Bronze II C, ca. 1650-1550) witnessed an influx of Kassites in Mesopotamia and Hyksos rule in Egypt.

§ *Late Bronze Age.* ca. 1550-1200 B.C. Egypt's empire extended far and wide, dominating the city-states of Syria-Palestine. Her chief competitor was the Hittite empire of Anatolia. Mesopotamia was experiencing "dark ages" initiated by the Kassites. Egyptian texts from the Late Bronze Age, primarily the Amarna Letters and monumental inscriptions from the XVIII-XIX dynasties, provide our earliest written information of consequence (except for the Bible) pertaining to the Holy Land. We learn, for example, that most of the major cities were situated in the lowlands (coastal plain, Jezreel Valley) and ruled by governors subject to Egypt. A royal inscription from the reign of Merneptah (ca. 1236-1223) includes the earliest non-biblical reference to Israel—and the only such reference earlier than the ninth century B.C.

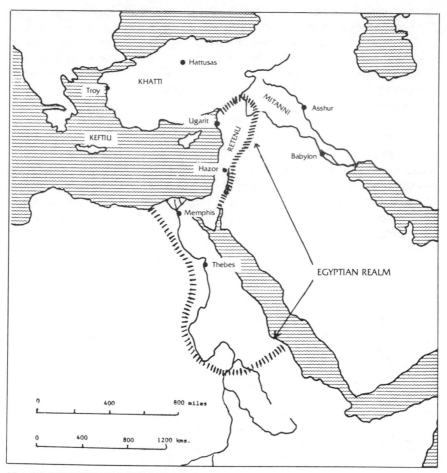

Map 24: EGYPTIAN EMPIRE DURING THE REIGN OF TUTHMOSE III (ca. 1482-1450)

Iron Age: Old Testament Times. The Iron Age represents the third millennium of recorded history in the Middle East and was the time of the Old Testament kings and prophets. Archaeologists recognize three sub-divisions: Iron I, Iron II, and the Persian Period. These subdivisions correspond to biblical history as follows:

§ *Iron I* (ca. 1200-925 B.C.). The Egyptian empire, which had dominated Syria-Palestine throughout the late Bronze Age, was in decline. This allowed several small local kingdoms to emerge in the Holy Land: Edom, Moab, Israel, Ammon, Philistia and Phoenicia. Ammon was an expanded city-state for all practical purposes, consisting of the city Rabbah and its surrounding territory. Philistia was a coalition of five Philistine cities (Asdod, Ashkelon, Gaza, Ekron, Gath) situated along the coastal plain south of where Tel Aviv stands today. Phoenicia consisted of several essentially independent cities (Tyre, Sidon, Byblos and others) situated along the coast further north.

During the first two centuries of the Iron Age, we find the Israelite tribes scattered without a king in the central hill country and Galilee with enclaves in Transjordan (ca. 1200-1000 B.C.; see the book of Judges). Then, under the leadership of Samuel, Saul and David, an Israelite monarchy was established which remained intact for approximately three-quarters of a century (ca. 1000-925 B.C.; see 1-2 Samuel). This was the kingdom over which Solomon ruled (1 Kings 1-11). Exact dates for the various judges, Samuel, Saul, David and Solomon cannot be established with certainty. It should be noted, moreover, that, while the splendor of Solomon's realm must have been impressive by local standards of the day, both the details of the biblical account and the archaeological record suggest that his kingdom really was very modest compared to the ancient empires of Egypt, Anatolia and Mesopotamia.

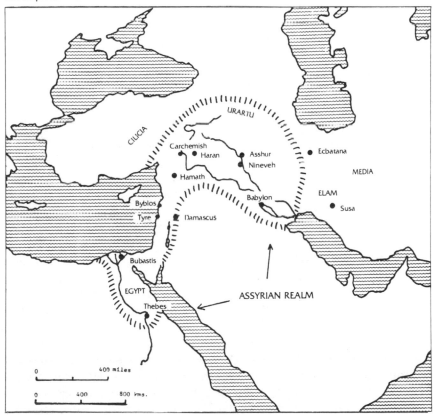

Map 25: ASSYRIAN EMPIRE DURING THE SEVENTH CENTURY B.C.

§ *Iron II* (ca. 925-539). After Solomon's death the Israelite monarchy was split into two separate Israelite kingdoms: one centered in the northern part of the central hill country that retained the name "Israel"; the other, called "Judah," centered in the southern part of the central hill country (See 1 Kings 12). These two kingdoms continued alongside the other local city-states and kingdoms of the Holy Land until they were engulfed by the Assyrian and Babylonian empires. Specifically, Israel, the northern kingdom, fell to the Assyrians in 722 B.C. (2 Kings 17). Judah, the southern kingdom, was conquered by the Babylonians in 597 and 586 B.C. (2 Kings 24-25; Jeremiah 52). In accordance with their practice, the Babylonians transported the aristocracy and officials of Judah to Mesopotamia where they could be kept under close surveillance. This was the so-called "Babylonian exile."

§ *Persian Period* (539-333 B.C.). Cyrus the Great founded a Persian empire which dominated the Middle East for two centuries. One of his first official acts after conquering Babylon, in 539 B.C., was to release the exiles from various nations which the Babylonians had interned in Mesopotamia. Some of the exiled Jews returned to Judah and, over a period of time, restored Jerusalem and rebuilt the Temple. This was the so-called "post-exilic period" of biblical history. Leading figures were Zerubbabel, Ezra, Nehemiah, Haggai and Zechariah.

Hellenistic Period: Between the Testaments. After the battle of Issus in 333 B.C., the whole Persian empire fell quickly into Alexander's hands. Pushing still further to the east, he soon was master of all the lands between upper Egypt and India. Following his death in 323 B.C., Alexander's eastern territories were divided between two officers, Ptolemy and Seleucus. Ptolemy received Egypt, Seleucus received Mesopotamia, and they established dynasties in their respective realms. For the next two and a half centuries the Holy Land was disputed territory between the Ptolemies and Seleucids. Finally, during the latter half of the second century B.C., an independent Jewish kingdom emerged which was centered in Jerusalem and ruled by the Hasmoneans.

§ *Ptolemies and Seleucids.* Ptolemy I seized the Holy Land and much of Syria in spite of the claims of Seleucus I that these territories rightly belonged to him. Ptolemy II strengthened the Ptolemaic grip with two major wars: the so-called First Syrian War (274-271 B.C.) fought against Antiochus I and the Second Syrian War (263-260 B.C.) against Antiochus II. The records of Zenon, one of Ptolemy II's officials who traveled extensively in the Holy Land, provides much useful information about local circumstances and conditions at this time.

Ptolemy III defended the Ptolemaic hold on the Holy Land with a Third

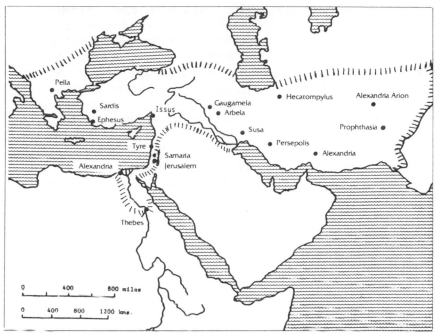

Map 26: CONQUESTS OF PHILIP AND ALEXANDER THE GREAT

Syrian War (246-241 B.C.) fought against Seleucus II. The people of Jerusalem seem to have favored the Seleucids during this war. Especially influential in Judean politics about this time was the Tobiad family from Transjordan. A Fourth Syrian War (221-217 B.C.) broke out during the reign of Ptolemy IV, with the Ptolemaic armies once again able to maintain their grip on the Holy Land.

Ptolemy V came to the Egyptian throne as a minor and was no match for Antiochus III, who had been ruling the Seleucid kingdom already for twenty years. By 198 B.C., as the result of decisive battles fought at Paneas and Gaza, all of Syria and the Holy Land was in Seleucid hands. Antiochus III continued to expand his kingdom until his interests began to conflict with those of Rome and eventually he was defeated by the Romans at Magnesia (in Greece) in 189 B.C. Hannibal was with Antiochus at Magnesia, having escaped to the Seleucid court after his own defeat by the Romans at Zama in 202 B.C.

The Seleucid line continued to rule in Syria until Pompey's invasion in 64 B.C. Cleopatra VII, the one remembered for her association with Julius Caesar and Marc Antony, was the last of the Ptolemaic line in Egypt.

§ *Maccabean Rebellion and Hasmonean dynasty.* Antiochus IV attempted to impose Hellenistic culture, including the worship of Zeus, on his subjects. This resulted in a successful Jewish rebellion initiated by Mattathias, an elderly priest from the village of Modein. The rebellion was led by Mattathias' three sons (Judas, Jonathan, and Simon) and is described in the book of I Maccabees. Judas was called the "Maccabi," which means "hammer," because of his guerrilla military tactics; and the rebellion, which broke out ca. 166 B.C., is usually referred to as the Maccabean Rebellion. Judas conquered Jerusalem in 164 and cleansed the temple, an event which is celebrated by Jews each year on Hanukkah.

Judas' taking of Jerusalem did not mean that the struggle was completed. A garrison of Seleucid soldiers remained ensconced in the Acra, a secondary fort inside the city. Moreover, not all of Judas' countrymen had favored rebellion in the first place. When Judas fell in battle in 160 B.C., therefore, a pro-Seleucid party seized the temple. Jonathan reorganized the resistance, accomplished a decisive victory over the Seleucid army (led by Bacchides) and was installed as high priest in the Jerusalem temple at the Feast of Tabernacles in 153 B.C. He thus became the official head of a Jewish kingdom and founder of the Hasmonean dynasty. Under John Hyrcanus (135/34-104 B.C.) and Alexander Jannaeus (103-76 B.C.), the Hasmoneans extended their realm to include most of the Holy Land.

Roman Period: The Rise and Spread of Christianity. Pompey invaded Syria in 64 B.C., conquered the Seleucids, and annexed their territory to the Roman empire. It now became the Roman province of Syria. The following year he marched on Jerusalem and settled a Hasmonean throne dispute in favor of Hyrcanus II. While confirming Hyrcanus as high priest in place of Aristobulus II, however, Pompey reduced the size of the Hasmonean realm significantly and made it tributary to Rome. The coastal cities, Samaria, Scythopolis and all the non-Jewish cities in the Transjordan were placed under the administration of the Roman governor of Syria. Scythopolis (the Beth Shean of Old Testament times) joined with Damascus and several Transjordan cities to form the Decapolis League. During the next two and a half centuries the Holy Land was part of the Roman empire and its history must be understood in the context of Roman history.

§ *The First Triumvirate (Caesar, Pompey, Crassus).* The Roman republic gave way to virtual dictatorship during the first century B.C. A decisive step was taken in that direction in 60 B.C., when Pompey, Caesar and Crassus joined in an agreement known as the First Triumvirate. Pompey was a famous general, having just returned from his conquests in the Middle East. Caesar was an ambitious politician who had won broad popular support. Crassus was a wealthy aristocrat who had largely financed Caesar's career. Combining their efforts, these three men were able to determine who would be consul and insure the consul's control over the Senate. They arranged for Caesar to be consul in 59 B.C. and then governor of Gaul from 58 to 50 B.C. Pompey and Crassus served as joint consuls from 55 to 52 B.C. and then Crassus died, leaving Pompey as sole consul.

By 50 B.C., when Caesar prepared to return to Rome for another term as consul, neither Pompey nor the senate wanted him back. Caesar returned with his army, therefore, a move which represented defiance of Roman political tradition. Crossing the Rubicon river, he marched on Rome and seized the city. Pompey and the senators attempted to raise an army and make a stand in Greece, but Caesar defeated them at Pharsalus in 48 B.C. Pompey fled to Egypt where he was murdered; Caesar ruled the Roman empire without opposition until his assassination in 44 B.C.

The Holy Land remained subject to Rome throughout this period—in fact two unsuccessful attempts by Aristobulus II and his son Alexander to stir up rebellion tended to strengthen Rome's grip. Antipater, who had supported Hyrcanus II in his claims to the Hasmonean throne, was also a friend and supporter of Caesar. Thus, as Caesar became increasingly powerful in Rome, Antipater became increasingly powerful in Judea. He was designated Prefect of Judea in 55 B.C. After Caesar defeated Pompey and the senators he became virtual ruler of the Holy Land at large. His two sons, Phasel and Herod, served as governors of Judea and Galilee respectively.

§ *The Second Triumvirate (Octavian, Antony, Lipidus).* Caesar's assassination in 44 B.C. gave rise to a Second Triumvirate composed of Marc Antony (who was serving as consul with Caesar at the time of the latter's death), Octavian (Caesar's grandnephew and adopted son) and Lepidus (second in command of Caesar's army). There were significant repercussions in Judea as well. Antipater, whose political career had been closely associated with Caesar's, was assassinated within the year. Soon after (40 B.C.), Antigonus, another son of Aristobulus II, captured Jerusalem with Parthian help and proclaimed a restoration of the Hasmonean line. Phasel was executed. Herod escaped, first to Petra and then to Rome via Egypt. In Rome, the Triumvirate proclaimed him King of Judea and sent him back with an army commanded by the general Sosius. Jerusalem fell to Sosius and Herod in 37 B.C.

§ *Julio-Claudian dynasty.* Octavian eventually displaced his two Second Triumvirate allies. The final showdown between him and Antony was the famous naval battle at Actium in 31 B.C. Octavian won a decisive victory; Antony and Cleopatra committed suicide. Herod supported Antony in the conflict and thus had to answer to Octavian when it was over. Octavian reconfirmed Herod on the throne of Judea nevertheless, and their respective reigns overlapped a quarter of a century: Herod (also called Herod the

Great) ruled from 37 to 4 B.C., Octavian (also called Caesar Augustus) was sole emperor of the whole Roman world from 31 B.C. to A.D. 14.

Octavian initiated the Julio-Claudian line of emperors which covered approximately a century and came to an end, for all practical purposes, with Nero. Herod proved to be as loyal to Octavian as he had been to Antony. Octavian in turn expanded Herod's kingdom until it included most of the Holy Land. At Herod's death his kingdom was divided among three of his surviving sons: Archelaus, Herod Antipas and Philip. Herod's descendants were not as successful as he had been in maintaining order. By the time of Nero's death in A.D. 68, the Holy Land was embroiled in the so-called First Jewish Revolt.

Herod's Kingdom Divided among His Sons

When Herod the Great died in 4 B.C., his kingdom was divided as follows among three of his surviving sons:

Archelaus - Designated ethnarch of Judea and Samaria which he ruled until exiled in A.D. 6. Thereafter Judea, Samaria and Idumea became a Roman province administered by procurators, among whom was Pontius Pilate (A.D. 26-31). See Matthew 27; Mark 15; Luke 23; John 18:28-19:22.

Herod Antipas - Designated tetrarch of Galilee and Perea which he ruled until A.D. 39 when he was exiled to Gaul. This was the Herod contemporary with Jesus, the one who married Herodius and executed John the Baptist. See Matthew 14:1-12; Mark 6:14-29; Luke 3:18-20.

Philip - Designated tetrarch of territories in northern Transjordan which he ruled until his death in A.D. 34. Built Caesarea Philippi. See Matthew 16:13; Mark 8:27.

---

§ *Flavian dynasty.* Nero was succeeded by Galba, Otho and Vitellius in rapid order. At that point (A.D. 69) Vespasian, who had been sent to the Holy Land to put down the Jewish Revolt and had already reconquered Galilee, returned to Rome and was proclaimed emperor. Thus began the brief Flavian dynasty which consisted of Vespasian and his two sons, Titus and Domitian.

§ *Era of "Good Emperors."* When Domitian fell to a conspiracy in A.D. 96, there was no obvious candidate available for the throne. Thus the choice fell into the hands of the Senate who selected Nerva. Thereafter the hereditary principle was discarded for almost a century, during which the Roman empire enjoyed relative peace and prosperity under four very able emperors: Trajan, Hadrian, Antonius Pius and Marcus Aurelius. The Holy Land was rocked by a second major Jewish revolt, the so-called Bar Kochba Revolt, during Hadrian's reign.

§ *A century of decline.* Marcus Aurelius was succeeded by his son Commodus, which represented a return to the hereditary principle for selecting emperors. It also marked the beginning of a century of poor emperors and serious decline of the empire—that is from Marcus Aurelius' death in A.D. 180 until Diocletian ascended the throne in A.D. 284. Christianity spread rapidly. Origen taught at Caesarea during this period, for example, and the emperor Decius attempted near the end of the period to eliminate Christianity with a persecution which lasted approximately one year (A.D. 250). The center of Jewish leadership and learning shifted to certain cities in Galilee (Usha, Beth She'arim, Sepphoris) and then to Tiberias.

§ *Diocletian and Constantine.* Diocletian (A.D. 284-305) restored stability for a time, reorganized the army, and made a second attempt to stamp out Christianity. Also, for administrative purposes, he divided the empire into two parts: the western empire to be administered from Rome and the eastern empire to be administered from Byzantium. Diocletian's abdication in A.D. 305 was followed by civil war. Constantine emerged victorious, first as ruler of the west in A.D. 312 and then, in 324, as emperor of the whole empire.

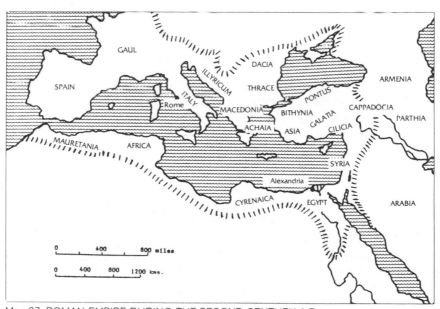

Map 27: ROMAN EMPIRE DURING THE SECOND CENTURY A.D.

Byzantine Period: Christianity as the Official Religion. Already in A.D. 313, the year after he became emperor of the western empire, Constantine issued the Edict of Milan jointly with Licinius. Licinius was emperor of the eastern empire at the time and the edict granted equal toleration to all religions of the Roman realm. In 325, the year after he displaced Licinius and became emperor of the eastern empire also, Constantine presided over the first International Christian Congress (at Nicea near the city of Byzantium). By the end of Constantine's reign Christianity was firmly established as the official religion of the Roman world.

Constantine chose Byzantium as his capital, renaming it Constantinople. After his death, the empire was once again split into two parts never to be joined together again. Byzantium/Constantinople continued to serve as capital of what had been the eastern Roman world (now the Byzantine Empire) until the Arab invasion in the seventh century. A remnant of the Byzantine Empire lingered on, in fact, until the city of Byzantium/Constantinople fell to the Ottoman Turks in 1453.

Thus, Byzantium dominated the Middle East for approximately 300 years, from Constantine to the Arab invasion. It was during this period that the early church hammered out its orthodox doctrinal positions at various church councils. The population of the Holy Land became almost entirely Christian, except for Jewish enclaves primarily in Galilee. Moreover, Chris-

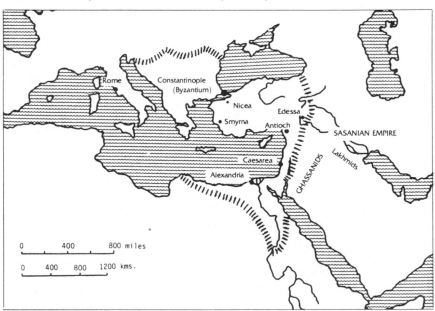

Map 28: BYZANTINE EMPIRE ON THE EVE OF THE RISE OF ISLAM

tian pilgrims flocked to the Holy Land from all over the Roman-Byzantium world and Christian churches were built over virtually every spot which could be imagined to have any connection with a biblical event.

Early Arab Period: Islam in Power. A.D. 622, the date of the "Hejira" (Mohammed's flight from Mecca to Medina), corresponds to year 1 of the Islamic calendar. The first clash between Muslim and Byzantine armies occurred seven years later (629) at Mauta in southern Transjordan. Although the Muslim army was defeated at Mauta, this defeat was only a temporary setback. In 636 (Mohammed had died in 632) the Arabs routed a Byzantine army near the Yarmuk River. By 640 most of Egypt, the Holy Land and Syria were under Islamic control.

This was hardly a conquest in the sense of overpowering indigenous peoples. Byzantine government of the seventh century was corrupt, its economic policies demoralizing, and the empire was fragmented by theological controversies. Large segments of the population had been declared "heretical" and were treated with intolerance. Once they achieved a few crucial victories over the Byzantine armies, therefore, the Arabs met with little resistance from the general population. By the end of the seventh century, the Arab realm included the Middle East (except for the much reduced Byzantine empire), North Africa, and much of Spain.

§ *The four "Rightly Guided Caliphs" (632-661).* After Mohammed's death, leadership of the Arab realm was in the hands of "caliphs" who traced their ancestry to Mohammed or his immediate family. The first four caliphs (Abu Bekr, Omar, Othman, and Ali) had been personally associated with Mohammed. They ruled from Medina and are referred to in Islam as the four "Rightly Guided Caliphs." It was under their leadership that Islam made its first rapid expansion in the Middle East.

§ *The Umayyad Caliphate (661-750).* Ali's election to follow Othman as caliph was opposed by the powerful Umayya family. Civil war broke out and the Umayyads emerged victorious. The Umayyad caliphs chose to rule from Damascus and adopted much of Byzantine culture. Byzantine influence is especially apparent, for example, in Umayyad architecture. Among the Umayyad caliphs who undertook significant building activities in the Holy Land were Abd el-Malik, al-Walid, Suleiman and Hisham.

§ *The Abbasid Caliphate (750-969).* After the death of Hisham, the Umayyad empire declined rapidly and soon was split apart by tribal strife. Under these circumstances a party arose in the east (Mesopotamia and Persia) led by Mohammed ibn Ali ibn al-Abbas, who traced his ancestry to an uncle of Mohammed the prophet. Having established themselves in the east, the Abbasids swept rapidly westward, defeated the Umayyads, and became the new masters of the Arab world.

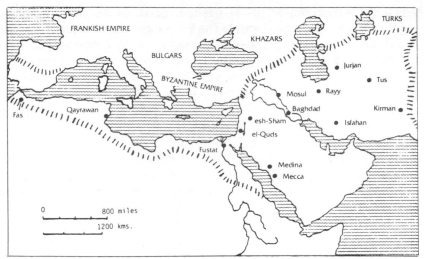

Map 29: MUSLIM LANDS AT THE TIME OF HARUN AL-RASHID (786-809)

The Abbasids chose Baghdad as their capital and introduced a period of flowering for Islamic culture (influenced now more by Persian than Byzantine styles). Achievements of this period found expression in new heights of learning and luxuriant court life. One of the Abbasid caliphs was Harun ar-Rashid (786-809), the famous caliph of the "thousand-and-one-nights." The Holy Land, no longer quite so near to the center of government, tended to be neglected.

§ *The Fatimid Caliphate (969-1171)*. The Abbasids were unable to maintain control of Spain, North Africa and Egypt. During the tenth century the Fatimid dynasty, Shi'ites who traced their ancestry to Fatima, Mohammed's daughter, established themselves in Cairo and soon became the real masters of the Holy Land and Syria. The Fatimids remained in power in Egypt until they were displaced by the Ayyubids (Saladin's dynasty) in 1171, but they had lost the Holy Land and Syria to the Seljuk Turks already in 1077.

Crusader Period: Seljuk Turks, Franks and Mongols. Seljuk Turks from central Asia invaded Mesopotamia, Syria and the Holy Land during the eleventh century (Damascus fell in 1055; Jerusalem in 1077). This posed a serious threat to the still-lingering Byzantine empire. In 1095, therefore, the Byzantine emperor Alexius Comnenus appealed to Pope Urban II for help. The appeal was timely: (1) Reports were reaching Europe that the Seljuks were molesting Christian pilgrims in the Holy Land, indeed that they had profaned the Church of the Holy Sepulchre; (2) Urban's claim to the papacy was under serious challenge—he needed a good "cause" which would rally the Roman church behind him; (3) The European nobles needed new lands to conquer. Thus Urban proposed a Crusade, a military expedition to invade the Holy Land and redeem the Holy Sepulchre from the "infidels." After some false starts (such as Peter the Hermit's dismal effort) an army of nobles and knights reached the Holy Land and took Jerusalem. Specifically, Jerusalem fell to the Crusaders in 1099, just thirty-three years after William the Conquerer invaded England. Muslims were slaughtered by the thousands, mercilessly and indiscriminately. Jews still living in the Holy Land were also regarded as infidels. Many of them fled to Egypt at this time.

§ *The Crusader Kingdom of Jerusalem (1099-1187).* Four Latin kingdoms were established in the Middle East as a result of this First Crusade (Edessa, Antioch, Tripoli and Jerusalem). Godfrey of Bouillon was elected "Defender of the Holy Sepulchre" by his fellow Crusaders when they conquered Jerusalem in 1099, and he defeated an Egyptian (Fatimid) army near Ashkelon the same year. Baldwin I was the real founder of the Kingdom of Jerusalem, however, in the sense that he established firm Crusader control over virtually all of the Holy Land. This Crusader kingdom of Jerusalem lasted for almost a hundred years, until 1187.

A dispute regarding the succession to the throne divided the Crusaders following Baldwin IV's death in 1185. Also, Renauld de Chatillon, lord of Le

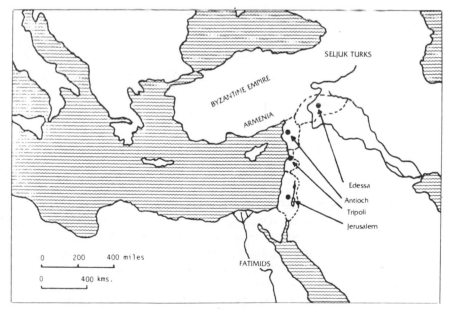

Map 30: FOUR CRUSADER KINGDOMS FOLLOWING THE FIRST CRUSADE

Crac (Kerak), very foolishly broke a truce with Saladin by attacking Muslim pilgrims on their way to Mecca. In 1187 Saladin met and crushed a combined Crusader army at the "Horns of Hattin" (between Nazareth and Tiberius). By the end of the year Jerusalem and all the coastal cities except Tyre were in Saladin's hands.

§ *The Later Crusades, Mongols and Mamluks (1187-1260)*. The Crusaders hung on tenaciously in the Holy Land for yet another century. Indeed six more Crusades were launched in hopes of restoring the Kingdom of Jerusalem. None of the later Crusades was entirely successful, however, and in 1260 the Holy Land became the scene of a desperate clash between the Mongols and Mamluks.

The great Mongol empire, founded by Genghis Khan in the thirteenth century, extended from China to eastern Europe. Shortly after Genghis Khan's death, Mongols conquered Baghdad (1258) and Damascus (1260). Their advance was halted by a Mamluk army at Ain Jalud in the Jezreel Valley, however, after which the Mamluks set about to expel the Crusaders from the Holy Land once and for all. The last five Crusader castles (Atlit, Acre, Tyre, Sidon and Beirut) fell in 1291. The Crusaders departed and the Mamluks instituted a "scorched earth" policy along the coast to prevent their return.

Mamluk Period. The Mamluks were slaves, most of them of Central Asian Turkish origin, trained for administrative and military service under the Ayyubids in Egypt. Gradually they became a privileged and powerful military caste, and after 1250 displaced the Ayyubid caliphs altogether. Baybars was the Mamluk general who defeated the Mongols at Ain Jalud in 1260. The same year he proclaimed himself sultan of Egypt. Mamluk sultans ruled Egypt and dominated the Holy Land for the next two and three-quarters centuries, until they were defeated by the Ottoman Turks in 1516. Even under Ottoman rule the Mamluks continued to be a powerful force in Egypt.

Ottoman Period. A horde of Ottoman Turks entered Asia Minor ca. 1300, on the heels of the Seljuks and Mongols. They crossed the Dardanelles in 1353 and soon were threatening Vienna. Byzantium/Constantinople fell to them in 1453, which they renamed Istanbul and established as their capital. In 1516 the Ottomans defeated the Mamluks in a decisive battle at Marj Dabiq (near Aleppo in northern Syria). The following year they conquered Egypt, thus bringing the Mamluk sultanate to an end and securing their hold on the Holy Land. The Ottomans reached their zenith under Suleiman "the Magnificent" (1520-1566) and dominated the Holy Land for four centuries—until World War I.

The Ottoman empire was divided for administrative purposes into "pashaliks" (districts), each governed by a "pasha" answerable to the

"Porte" in Istanbul. After Suleiman's reign the empire began to decline. By the eighteenth and nineteenth centuries, for example, many of the pashas and local sheikhs nominally within the Ottoman realm ruled independently of Istanbul for all practical purposes. Also, especially following Napoleon's invasion of Egypt and the Holy Land in 1798-1801, the Ottoman empire was increasingly at the mercy of the European nations and Russia. It was during these last two centuries of the Ottoman period that travelers and archaeologists began to explore systematically the antiquities of the Middle East. One might say, in fact, that the ancient world was rediscovered during the Ottoman period.

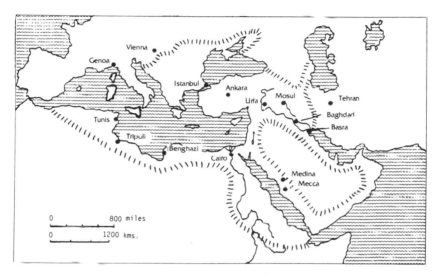

Map 31: OTTOMAN EMPIRE DURING THE SIXTEENTH CENTURY

Mandate Period and Following. World War I (1914-1918) brought to an end four centuries of Ottoman rule in the Holy Land, introduced a period of European domination of the Middle East through Mandate governments, and set the stage for the Arab-Israeli conflict which jeopardizes world peace today.

§ *World War I.* Following their successful challenge to Napoleon's invasion, the British established a strong presence in Egypt. At the outbreak of World War I, therefore, Britain proclaimed Egypt a protectorate and used it as a base of military operations against the Ottoman empire in the Middle East. The British foreign department also encouraged Hussein Ibn Ali, Sharif of Mecca, to initiate an Arab rebellion against the Turks (McMahon-Hussein letters, 1915). This encouragement involved what amounted to a promise of

Arab independence and autonomy in their own lands at the end of the war—a promise which conflicted with other promises being made at the same time. Specifically, the French were assured that their claim to most of Syria would be recognized (Sykes-Picot Agreement, 1916), while the Jews were led to believe that they would receive a portion of Palestine as a national homeland (Balfour Declaration, 1917).

§ *The Mandate Period (between the World Wars).* With the war over and the League of Nations established, some disposition now had to be made of the emancipated territories. The League of Nations adopted the "mandate" concept as a guiding principle, which was to satisfy neither the Arabs nor the Jews. The mandate divisions were worked out at the Peace Conference of San Remo in April, 1920 (although the final draft was not officially approved by the League of Nations until July, 1922). France received Syria as a mandate, including the interior with Damascus and what is present-day Lebanon. Britain received Mesopotamia and the Holy Land.

The Arab leaders who had participated in the rebellion against the Turks during the war considered this a breach of promise. Thus Abdullah, one of

Balfour Declaration

The so-called Balfour Declaration took the form of a letter written on November 2, 1917, by Arthur James Balfour, then Secretary of State for Foreign Affairs, and addressed to Lord Rothschild. This was the first formal indication of British support for a Jewish homeland in Palestine.

My dear Lord Rothschild,

I have much pleasure in conveying to you, on behalf of His Majesty's Government, the following declaration of sympathy with Jewish Zionist aspirations which has been submitted to, and approved by, the Cabinet.

"His Majesty's Government view with favor the establishment in Palestine of a national home for the Jewish people, and will use their best endeavours to facilitate the achievement of this object, it being clearly understood that nothing shall be done which may prejudice the civil and religious rights of existing non-Jewish communities in Palestine, or the rights and political status enjoyed by Jews in any other country."

I should be grateful if you would bring this declaration to the knowledge of the Zionist Federation.

Yours,
(signed)
A.W. James Balfour

Sharif Hussein's sons, collected a Bedouin army and marched north from Mecca into the Transjordan. As a result of the negotiations which followed, the British divided the Holy Land into two parts governed separately. The area west of the Jordan River was designated "Palestine" and administered directly by the British; Transjordan was designated as an emirate (kingdom) under British protection with Abdullah as its first emir. This situation continued until 1948 when Britain terminated the mandate government of Palestine, Israel proclaimed itself a nation, and the first Arab-Israeli war broke out.

§ *Israel and Jordan.* When the fighting ended with armistice agreements in 1949, the young nation Israel controlled a sizable portion of the territory west of the Jordan River. Excluded were the so-called Gaza Strip and West Bank. The Gaza Strip along with the Sinai Peninsula was in Egyptian hands; Abdullah's troops held the West Bank. In 1950, the people of the West Bank decided by referendum to join Abdullah's kingdom. Having finally gained independence from the British in 1946 and now including territory west of the Jordan River, the Emirate of Transjordan came to be called simply "Jordan" or the "Hashemite Kingdom of Jordan." Hostilities have continued between Israel and the surrounding Arab nations, with open warfare in 1956, 1967 and 1973. Israel gained military control of the Gaza Strip, West Bank (including East Jerusalem), and the Golan Heights as a result of the 1967 war.

Chronological Charts

EGYPTIAN PHARAOHS OF DYNASTY XVIII

Ancient Egypt enjoyed the height of her classical culture during the third millennium B.C. (the pyramids, etc.) As an empire, however, she reached her zenith during the late Bronze Age under the pharaohs of dynasty XVIII. These pharaohs resided at Thebes, in upper Egypt, and were buried in the so-called "Valley of the Kings." They dominated the Holy Land, especially following the conquests of Tuthmosis III, and installed vassal rulers in the major cities (Abdu-Heba of Jerusalem, for example; see "Letter from Abdu-Heba of Jerusalem," above, under "Deciphering Ancient Languages").

Amosis (ca. 1570-1546 B.C.)	Expelled the Hyksos from Egypt
Amenophis I (ca. 1546-1526)	Began to establish Egyptian authority in Nubia and Libya.
Tuthmosis I (ca. 1546-1512)	Campaigned in Nubia and Syria-Palestine as far as the Euphrates River. Built the core of the present structure of the Temple at Karnak. First Pharaoh to be buried in the "Valley of the Kings."
Tuthmosis II (ca. 1512-1504)	Gained the throne through marriage to Hatshepsut, daughter of Tuthmosis I. A weak ruler, dominated by Hatshepsut and the queen-mother.
Hatshepsut (ca. 1504-1482)	Undertook an extensive building program which included her famous mortuary temple at Deir el-Bahri and additions to the Temple at Karnak.
Tuthmosis III (ca. 1482-1450)	Son of Tuthmosis II by another wife than Hatshepsut, Tuthmosis III was one of the great conquerers of the ancient world. He conquered Syria-Palestine, for example, and left records of his campaigns which are extremely valuable to historians and archaeologists.
Amenophis II (ca. 1450-1425)	Was able to maintain the empire which Tuthmosis III had left. Two major campaigns into the Holy Land and Syria.

Tuthmosis IV (ca. 1425-1417)	Cleared the sphinx at Giza which had become covered with sand during the approximately 1,000 years since its construction by Pharaoh Kafre (ca. 2500 B.C.). Minor military campaigns.
Amenophis III (ca. 1417-1379)	Long peaceful reign with little need to engage in foreign wars. Erected impressive buildings and monuments including the temple at Luxor (later expanded by Rameses II) and a gigantic mortuary temple (of which only the so-called "Colossi of Memnon" remain).
Amenophis IV (ca. 1379-1362)	=Akhenaton. Undertook a religious reform designed to replace Amun (the traditional god of Thebes) with Aten (the sun disk) as the state religion. Built a new capital city in what is now the el-Amarna district of Egypt. The famous Amarna letters date from his reign and were discovered at the site of his capital.
Smenkhkare and Tutankhamen (ca. 1362-1352)	Smenkhkare and Tutankhamen, probably sons of Amenophis III, ruled each in turn for brief periods. Tutankhamen is the "King Tut" whose burial tomb (and treasure) was discovered in the "Valley of the Kings."
Eye (ca. 1352-1348)	An elderly royal advisor who ruled briefly following Tutankhamen.
Horemheb (ca. 1348-1320)	Another commoner who had been commander of the Army and probably the real power behind the throne as early as Tutankhamen's reign. Began the process of reestablishing control over the provinces which had been lost during Amenophis IV's reign and following. Further additions to the Temple of Karnak.

EGYPTIAN PHARAOHS OF DYNASTIES XIX-XX

The pharaohs of dynasties XIX attempted with decreasing success to restore and maintain the empire established by dynasty XVIII. Israel appears on the scene of recorded history at this time.

Rameses I (ca. 1320-1318 B.C.)	A commoner who had been raised to the rank of vizier by Horemheb and named his successor, Rameses established a dynasty which ruled Egypt for 100 years.
Sethos I (ca. 1318-1304)	Completed restoring Egyptian control over Nubia and the Holy Land. Began construction on the massive "hypostyle hall" at Karnak. Fragments of two inscriptions from Sethos' reign have been discovered by archaeologists at Beth-shean.
Rameses II (ca. 1304-1237)	Reconquered southern Syria, but was halted by the Hittites at the famous battle of Kadesh on the Orontes River. An inscription from his reign was discovered at Beth-shean, and three more inscriptions at the mouth of the Dog River in Lebanon. Undertook an extensive building program,

including the northeast section of the temple at Luxor, the famous temple at Abu Simbel, and completion of the "hypostyle hall" at Karnak. Some scholars believe him to have been the pharaoh of the Hebrew exodus (Exodus 1:11).

Merneptah
(ca. 1236-1223)

Thirteenth son of Rameses II and already advanced in years when he ascended the throne. Fought a major battle against Libyan tribes, which he commemorated with an inscribed stele erected at Thebes. Near the end of the inscription, after recounting his victory over the Libyans, Merneptah claims to have put down disturbances in Palestine as well. He mentions "Israel" in this context; this is the oldest known reference to Israel in any non-biblical document.

(ca. 1223-1206)

Disputes regarding succession to the throne disrupted order for approximately the next 20 years. Finally order was restored by a man of unknown origin named Sethnakht. His successors, the pharaohs of dynasty XX, all of whom adopted "Rameses" as their throne name, moved the seat of government from Thebes in Upper Egypt to Avaris-Tanis in the Delta. Egypt's day of glory had passed. Only one pharaoh of this dynasty deserves special mention.

Rameses III
(ca. 1206-1175)

Son of Sethnakht; protected Egypt against onslaught of the "sea peoples," among whom were the Philistines. Rameses III sought to imitate Rameses II, and was the last great builder of ancient Egypt.

RULERS OF THE TWO ISRAELITE KINGDOMS

During the first two centuries of the Iron Age (ca. 1200-1000 B.C.) we find essentially autonomous Israelite tribes scattered throughout the Holy Land. The narratives in the book of Judges relate to this period, which Judges 21:25 describes as a time when "there was no king in Israel and every man did what was right in his own eyes." Then, under the leadership of Samuel, Saul and David who lived ca. 1000 B.C., an Israelite monarchy was established (described in 1-2 Samuel). This was the kingdom over which Solomon enjoyed a long and prosperous reign (1 Kings 1-11). Following Solomon's death, the monarchy was split into two smaller kingdoms: a northern kingdom called "Israel" with its capital at Samaria, and a southern kingdom called "Judah" with its capital at Jerusalem.

Kings of Judah	Kings of Israel		
Rehoboam	Jeroboam I	924 B.C.	
Abijah		907	
Asa		905	Half a century of hostilities between the two kingdoms. (See esp. 1 Kings 12-16)
	Nadab	904	
	Baasha	903	
	Elah	886	
	Zimri, Tibni	885	

	Omri	885	Omride dynasty. Marriage alliance between the two kingdoms (1 Kings 16-2 Kings 10). The prophets Elijah and Elisha active at this time.
Jehoshaphat		875	
	Ahab	874	
	Ahaziah	852	
Jehoram		851	Ashurnasirpal II (853-859)
	Jehoram	850	Shalmaneser III (858-824)*

Ahaziah, Athaliah	Jehu	842	Period of oppression by the Aramaean kings of Damascus: Hazael and Ben-hadad (2 Kings 10:32-13:25). Elisha still active.
Jehoash		837	
	Jehoahaz	815	
	Joash	801	Shamshi-adad (823-811)
Amaziah		800	Adad-nirari III (810-783)*

	Jeroboam II	786	A brief moment of national recovery (2 Kings 14:1-15:7). Amos, Hosea
Azariah = Uzziah		783	Shalmaneser IV (782-773)
			Ashur-dan (772-756)
			Ashur-nirari V (755-745)

Jotham (regent)		750	
	Zechariah	746	
	Shallum, Menahem	745	Assyrian domination of Syria-Palestine. With the fall of Samaria ca. 722, the northern kingdom ceases to exist as an independent kingdom (2 Kings 15:8-21:26). Isaiah, Micah
Jotham (king)		742	
	Pekahiah	738	
	Pekah	737	
Jehoahaz I		735	Tiglath-pileser III (744-727)*
	Hoshea	732	Shalmaneser V (726-722)
	Fall of Samaria	722/1	Sargon II (721-705)*
			Sennacherib (704-681)*
			Esarhaddon (680-669)*
Hezekiah		715	
Manasseh		687	
Amon		642	

Josiah		640	Judah recovers her independence for a brief moment under Josiah, but soon is firmly in the hands of Egypt (under Necho) and then Babylon (2 Kings 22-24:1). Zephaniah, Jeremiah, Nahum, Habakkuk, Ezekiel.
Jehoahaz II		609	
Jehoiakim		609	
Jehoiachin		598	
First Surrender of Jerusalem		597	
Zedekiah		597	Nabopolassar (626-604)*
Destruction of Jerusalem		586	Nebuchadrezzar (604-561)*

*Records pertaining to the reigns of these Mesopotamian kings make references to certain of the Israelite and Judean kings, thus allowing some fairly close chronological correlations. Fortunately, the Mesopotamian kings can be dated in terms of the Gregorian calendar.

ASSYRIAN AND BABYLONIAN RULERS

Ashur, a city-state in the Mesopotamian Valley, emerged during the ninth century B.C. as a major empire and dominated the Fertile Crescent for the next 200 years. When the Assyrian Empire collapsed near the end of the seventh century, its role as head of nations fell to another Mesopotamian city-state, Babylon. Among the smaller nations of the Fertile Crescent which found themselves in the grips of first Assyria and then Babylon were the two Israelite kingdoms, Israel and Judah.

Assyrian rulers

Ashurnasirpal II (883-859 B.C.)	The Assyrian Empire began its ascent under Ashurnasirpal II. He built impressive palaces—for example at Calah (present-day Nimrud) which began to replace Ashur as the Assyrian capital.
Shalmaneser III (858-824)	Continued to expand Assyria's territories in all directions with numerous military campaigns. In 853 he engaged a coalition of Syro-Palestinian kings at a place called Qarqar on the Orontes River. Among these kings, whom he named in a royal inscription, was Ahab of Israel (1 Kings 16:28 ff.). Later Shalmaneser would fight against Hazael of Damascus and collect tribute from Jehu (2 Kings 8:28 ff.).
Shamshi-Adad V (823-811)	Campaigned against Urartu and Media, nations to the north and east of Mesopotamia respectively. Also found it necessary to put down revolts among the Chaldeans of southern Mesopotamia.
Adad-nirari III (810-783)	Adad-nirari was still a child when his father died, so Assyria was ruled for four years by his mother, Sammuramat (the Semiramis of Greek legend). When Adad-Nirari began to rule for himself, he led Assyrian armies again in the direction of Syria-Palestine. A recently discovered inscription from his reign records that he received tribute from Joash of Israel (2 Kings 13:10-24).
Shalmaneser IV (782-773) Ashur-dan III (772-756) Ashur-nirari IV (755-745)	Assyria's military strength was directed primarily to the north (Urartu), east (Media) and south (Babylon and Chaldean tribes) during the reign of Shalmaneser IV and his two successors. Actually this was a period of relative weakness for Assyria. Some of the battles were clearly defensive.

Tiglath-pileser III (744-727)	Called "Pul" in the Old Testament (2 Kings 15:19 ff.), Tiglath-pileser was Assyria's most successful conquerer. The whole Fertile Crescent was firmly under Assyrian control by the end of his reign. Royal Assyrian inscriptions indicate that he collected tribute from Menahem of Israel (2 Kings 15:17 ff.) and Jehoahaz of Judah (= Ahaz; 2 Kings 16:1 ff.).
Shalmaneser V (726-722)	Relatively little is known about this king's reign. Apparently he conquered Samaria, which meant the end of the northern Israelite kingdom (2 Kings 17:3 ff.), although Sargon II actually claimed the credit.
Sargon II (721-705)	Active military career. Claimed many conquests, including the city of Samaria and all the land of Israel (which is normally referred to in the Assyrian records as "the land of the House of Omri"; see 1 Kings 16:21 ff.). Built Dur Sharrukin (present-day Khorsabad) as a new royal residence and capital for the empire.
Sennacherib (704-681)	Sennacherib moved the capital to Nineveh (present-day Kuyunjik), destroyed Babylon, and in 701 B.C., put down a revolt by Hezekiah of Judah (2 Kings 18:9 ff.; Isaiah 36-37). The Assyrian empire reached its furthermost extent and enjoyed relative stability under Sennacherib, Esarhaddon and Ashurbanipal.
Esarhaddon (680-669)	Active military career which involved the capture of Sidon and conquest of lower Egypt. Memphis fell to his army in 671 B.C. Manasseh of Judah appears to have been a thoroughly loyal vassal (2 Kings 21).
Ashurbanipal	Probably identical with Osnapper mentioned in Ezra 4:10, best remembered for the royal library which he collected at Nineveh. Ashurbanipal's armies plundered Thebes in 663 B.C. (called "No" in Nahum 3:8-10). As his reign drew to a close he had to struggle increasingly to maintain the empire.

The Assyrian empire declined rapidly after Ashurbanipal's death, while Babylon, under the energetic rule of Nabopolassar, emerged as a major power. Babylon had already enjoyed a peak of political and cultural influence among the people of the Fertile Crescent during the Middle Bronze Age (under Hammurabi).

Babylonian rulers

Nabopolassar (626-604)	Of Chaldean ancestry, he declared Babylon independent of Assyria in 625 B.C. Then, allied with the Medes, he conquered the Assyrian cities each in turn (between 615 and 612 B.C.; the biblical book Nahum celebrates the fall of Nineveh in 612). Ashuruballit, the Assyrian king, attempted a last desperate stand at Harran on the upper Euphrates and Pharaoh Neco II rushed to his support with an Egyptian army. Neco apparently clashed with a Judean army at

Megiddo along the way resulting in the death of King Josiah of Judah (2 Kings 23:29-30). Harran fell to Nabopolassar (609 B.C.) in spite of Neco's efforts and Neco himself was defeated decisively at Carchemish in 605.

Nebuchadrezzar II
(604-561)

Chaldean Babylon was now undisputed heir of Assyria's conquests. Nebuchadrezzar consolidated and maintained the empire, which finally involved the destruction of Jerusalem and an end to the kingdom of Judah (2 Kings 24-25; Jeremiah 39:1 ff.). This was the beginning of the so-called "Babylonian exile" of the Jews. Nebuchadrezzar's military successes were more than matched by his peaceful achievements. He rebuilt Babylon, for example, making it one of the wonders of the ancient world.

Amel-marduk
(561-559)

The next Babylonian kings (Nebuchadrezzar's son, son-in-law, and grandson) had brief and not very illustrious reigns.

Nergal-shar-usur
(559-555)

Labashi-marduk
(555)

Nabonidus
(555-539)

Favored the god Sin and spent most of his time at centers of Sin worship (Harran, Ur, and Tema in Arabia). This alienated the people of Babylon, especially the priests of Marduk, the chief god of the city. Eventually they turned against Belshazzar, whom Nabonidus had left in charge, and delivered the city over to Cyrus the Persian (539 B.C.).

PERSIAN RULERS

The Holy Land was a part of the Persian empire for two centuries. This was the so-called "post-exilic period" of biblical history.

Cyrus
(538-529 B.C.)

Allowed the exiles to return to Judah. Jeshua and Zerubbabel were active during his reign (see Ezra 1:1; 3:1-9).

Cambyses
(529-521)

Darius
(521-485)

Rebuilding of the Second Temple began during the 2nd and/or 6th year of Darius' reign (520/515 B.C.), apparently at the urging of Haggai and Zechariah (Ezra 4:24, 6:15, 19; Haggai 1:1, 15; 2:1, 10; Zechariah 1:1, 7; 7:1). Darius' expedition against Athens was halted with the battle of Marathon in 490 B.C.

Xerxes
(485-464)

Another Persian attempt to conquer Greece ended with the defeat of Xerxes' fleet at Salamas in 480 B.C.

Artaxerxes
(464-423)

This was the age of Pericles, the building of the Parthenon in Athens, and of Herodotus' travels. Ezra and Nehemiah returned to Jerusalem during the 7th and 12th years, respectively, of Artaxerxes' reign (458/455; see Ezra 7:1-10 and Nehemiah 1:1 ff.). It is possible that Ezra's career should be associated with the reign of Artaxerxes II rather than Artaxerxes I. The 7th year of Artaxerxes II would be 398.

Xerxes II
(423)

Assassinated.

Darius II
(423-404)

Strengthened Persia's grasp on Asia Minor. Peloponnesian War was underway between Sparta and Athens.

Artaxerxes II
(404-358)

Forced to deal with widespread revolts—e.g., Egypt and Asia Minor. The revolt in Asia Minor, led by a brother, was the setting of Xenophon's *Anabasis*.

Artaxerxes III
(358-337)

Reconquered Egypt, but Persian empire was beginning to fall apart.

Arses
(337-335)

Poisoned, and all his children killed in palace intrigues.

Darius III
(335-330)

Alexander the Great defeated Darius' army at Issus in 333 B.C.

PTOLEMAIC, SELEUCID, AND HASMONEAN RULERS

When Alexander died in 323, his eastern empire was divided between two high ranking officials. Ptolemy received Egypt and his descendants, the "Ptolemaic dynasty," ruled there until Cleopatra's death in 31 B.C. Seleucus received northern Syria and Mesopotamia where his descendants, the Seleucids, ruled until Pompey's invasion in 64 B.C. The Holy Land fell first into Ptolemaic hands, then into Seleucid hands. Eventually there emerged an independent Jewish kingdom centered in Jerusalem and ruled by the Hasmonean dynasty.

Ptolemaic rulers (Egypt)		Seleucid rulers (Mesopotamia)
Ptolemy I (323-285 B.C.)		Seleucus I (312-280)
Ptolemy II (285-246)	First Syrian War (274-271)	Antiochus I (280-261)
	Second Syrian War (260-253)	Antiochus II (261-247)
Ptolemy III (246-221)	Third Syrian War (246-241)	Seleucus II (247-226)
		Seleucus III (226-223)
Ptolemy IV (221-203)	Fourth Syrian War (221-217)	Antiochus III (223-187)
. . .		Seleucus IV (187-175)
		Antiochus IV (175-163)
		. . .

Hasmonean rulers
Judas Maccabaeus (166-160)
Jonathan (160-142)
Simeon (142-135/34)
John Hyrcanus (135/34-104)
Aristobulus (104-103)
Alexander Jannaeus (103-76)
Alexandra (76-67)
Aristobulus II/Hyrcanus II

Cleopatra VII, the last Ptolemaic ruler, committed suicide after Marc Antony's defeat at Actium in 31 B.C.

Pompey invaded Syria in 64 B.C. bringing the Seleucid kingdom to an end. The following year he settled a dispute between Aristobulus II and Hyrcanus II, both of whom claimed the Hasmonean throne. Pompey favored Hyrcanus, but left him ruler over a Judean kingdom much reduced in size and tributary to Rome.

HASMONEAN DYNASTY

(Beginning with the Maccabean Rebellion, ca. 166 B.C.)

Judas "the Maccabi"
(ca. 166-153 B.C.)

Mattathias died soon after initiating a Jewish rebellion against Antiochus IV and leadership of the rebellion fell to Judas, one of Mattathias's several sons. Judas was able to take Jerusalem in 164 and cleansed the Temple.

Jonathan
(153-142)

Judas was killed in battle in 160 B.C. and leadership fell next to his brother Jonathan. Jonathan accomplished a decisive victory over the Seleucid general Bacchides and was installed as High Priest at the Feast of Tabernacles in 153. Not all the Jews accepted this move. The Essenes, for example, who established a religious community at Qumran and left the Dead Sea Scrolls, may have withdrawn from worshipping at the Temple at this time.

Simeon
(142-135/34)

A third brother; conquered Gezer and succeeded in expelling the Seleucid garrison from the Acra. Antiochus VII (138-129 B.C.) then reconquered Jerusalem and restored Seleucid authority in the Holy Land.

John Hyrcanus
(135/34-104)

Simeon's son; restored Judean independence and expanded the Hasmonean realm to include virtually all of the territory west of the Jordan as well as parts of the Transjordan. Employed a policy of "conversion by force." Incurred the hatred of the Samaritans when he destroyed their temple on Mount Gerizim.

Aristobulus I
(104-103)

Hyrcanus's son; held the throne only temporarily in a power struggle with his brother, Alexander Jannaeus.

Alexander Jannaeus
(103-76)

Annexed more of the Transjordan to the Hasmonean kingdom. Among other victories, he conquered Gadara, Pella and Gerasa.

Salome Alexandra
(76-67)

Widow of Alexander Jannaeus; developed a strong alliance with the Pharisees to the extent that they became a powerful force in Hasmonean politics.

Aristobulus II
(67-63)

At Salome's death a power struggle ensued between Aristobulus and Hyrcanus, two sons which she had born to Alexander Jannaeus. Aristobulus defeated Hyrcanus and ascended the throne as Aristobulus II. Antipater, governor of Idumea, continued to support Hyrcanus' claim, however, and secured the support of Aretas, king of Nabatea.

Hyrcanus II
(63-40)

The dispute remained unsettled when Pompey invaded Syria in 64 B.C. He marched on Jerusalem the following year and placed Hyrcanus II on the throne. From that time on the rulers of Judea were answerable to Rome.

ROMAN RULERS

For almost four centuries (from Pompey's march on Jerusalem in 63 B.C. to Constantine's reign in the fourth century A.D.) Judea was part of the Roman empire. The following is a chronology of Roman rulers during this period with specific attention to circumstances and events in the Holy Land.

The First Triumvirate (Caesar, Pompey, Crassus; 60-48 B.C.)
Caesar (48-44 B.C.)
The Second Triumvirate (Octavian, Antony, Lipidus; 44-31 B.C.)
Julio-Claudian dynasty

Octavian (31 B.C.-A.D. 14)	Also called Caesar Augustus. Herod the Great was his contemporary and ruled under his authority. The Gospel of Luke begins its account of Jesus' birth as follows: "In those days a decree went out from Caesar Augustus that all the world should be enrolled. . . ."
Tiberias (A.D. 14-37)	Jesus' ministry occurred during the reign of Tiberias. Herod Antipas was tetrarch of Galilee. Judea was governed by procurators.
Caligula (A.D. 37-41)	Herod Agrippa, a grandson of Herod the Great, was educated in Rome where he became a close friend of Caligula. When Caligula became emperor he made Herod king of Galilee, Perea and portions of the Transjordan.
Claudius (A.D. 41-54)	Claudius extended Agrippa's realm to include all that had belonged to Herod the Great. When Agrippa died, his son, Agrippa II, was made king over parts of Galilee and Perea. Judea reverted to procurator rule, beginning with Felix (A.D. 52-60) and Festus (A.D. 60-62). The Apostle Paul's case was argued before Felix, Festus and Agrippa II (Acts 24-26).
Nero (A.D. 54-68)	Nero's persecution of the Christians appears to have been a temporary and self-serving move rather than than a systematic attempt to stamp out the movement. The First Jewish revolt broke out in Caesarea and quickly spread throughout the Holy Land. Vespasian was sent to put down the revolt.

Flavian dynasty

Vespasian (A.D. 69-79)	Galba, Otho and Vitellius, who succeeded Nero each in turn, were unable to hold the throne. Thus Vespasian returned to Rome and was proclaimed emperor. Titus, Vespasian's son whom he had left in charge of the military action against the Jewish revolt, conquered Jerusalem in A.D. 70. This meant the end of the Jewish Revolt for all practical purposes. Silva was appointed military governor with the responsibility of reducing the few remaining rebel strongholds. Masada was the last to fall (A.D. 73).
Titus (A.D. 79-81)	Titus' triumval arch in Rome depicts the Romans looting the Jerusalem Temple.

Domitian (A.D. 81-96)	Domitian combined the Decapolis cities with Perea in A.D. 90 to form the administrative province of Arabia.

Era of "Good Emperors"

Nerva (A.D. 96-98)	Elected by the Senate to follow Domitian, who had no obvious successor.
Trajan (A.D. 98-117)	Trajan annexed Nabatea to the province of Arabia in A.D. 106 and renamed the province Arabia Petraea. Work was begun on a new highway, the Via Nova, which would connect Damascus with the Red Sea and other points south. In A.D. 115-117 Jewish uprisings broke out in Cyrenaica, Egypt, Cyprus and Asia Minor, with some minor disturbances in the Holy Land.
Hadrian (A.D. 117-138)	Hadrian's visit to the eastern provinces in A.D. 129 was received with great fanfare. Wealthy citizens of Gerasa (Jerash) and Petra erected triumval arches. His plan to rebuild Jerusalem in grand Roman style incited a second major Jewish revolt in the Holy Land, supported by Rabbi Akiba and led by Simeon Bar Kochba (Kosiba). This is usually referred to as the Bar Kochba Revolt. The revolt was crushed, Judaism virtually wiped out in the southern part of the Holy Land, and Hadrian followed through with his plan to rebuild Jerusalem. He renamed the city Aelia Capitolina and forbade Jews to enter.
Antonius Pius (A.D. 138-161)	
Marcus Aurelius (A.D. 162-180)	The cities along the Via Nova in Transjordan flourished. For example, the temple on the citadel in Amman dates from the reign of Marcus Aurelius.

A Century of Decline

. . .

Diocletian (A.D. 284-305)

Constantine (A.D. 324-337)

IMPORTANT DATES, PEOPLE, AND EVENTS
FROM THE BYZANTINE PERIOD

The Holy Land was part of an empire centered at Byzantium for approximately 300 years—from the reign of Constantine to the Arab conquest. The following are some important dates, people and events from the Byzantine period:

A.D. 325	Council of Nicea sponsored by Constantine, followed by the founding of numerous churches in the Holy Land (Church of the Nativity, Church of the Holy Sepulchre).
ca. 313-340	Eusebius bishop of Caesarea.
361-363	Reign of Julian "the Apostate," Constantine's nephew, who attempted to restore paganism as the state religion.
ca. 348-420	Jerome resided near the Church of the Nativity in Bethlehem and translated the Vulgate. Ambrose (ca. 340-397) and Augustine (ca. 354-430).
381	Council of Constantinople (doctrine of the Trinity completed).
431	Council of Ephesus (Nestorian controversy: Nestorius condemned, which alienated much of the Syrian church).
451	Council of Chalcedon (Monophysite controversy: Patriarch of Alexandria condemned, which alienated Egyptian Christians. The Coptic, Ethiopian, Syrian/Jacobite and Armenian churches separated at this time).
527-565	Justinian I, a vigorous supporter of orthodox Christianity, directed another surge of Christian building activities (restoration of the Church of the Nativity, founding of St. Sophia in Constantinople and St. Catherine's monastery at the traditional site of Mt. Sinai). Samaritans and Jews revolted under Christian oppression.
614-628	Persian conquest of the Holy Land and recapture of the land by the Byzantines. The Persians systematically destroyed most of the Christian churches. The Church of the Nativity was spared, however, apparently because of its mosaics depicting the wise men from the East.

EARLY ARAB CALIPHATES

The Early Arab period began during the seventh century A.D. with the initial expansion of Islam and continued until the eleventh century when the Middle East was invaded in turn by Seljuk Turks and European Crusaders. After Mohammed's death in A.D. 632 the Arab world was ruled by caliphs.

The "Hegira" = year 1 of the Islamic calendar (A.D. 622)

The Four "Rightly Guided Caliphs" (A.D. 632-661)

Abu Bekr (632-634)	Mohammed's father-in-law. He put down revolts in Arabia and conquered southern Mesopotamia.
Omar (634-644)	Head of the Islamic army, which elected him Caliph at Abu Bekr's death. Defeated the Byzantines near the Yarmuk River (636); conquered Jerusalem and Caesarea (637). By 640 he had extended Islamic control over virtually all of the Holy Land, Egypt and Syria.
Othman (644-656)	Member of the Umayya family and strongly influenced by the old Meccan Aristocracy. Political opposition resulted in a rebellion and his murder.
Ali (656-661)	Married to Fatima, Mohammed's daughter, Ali was elected to follow Othman. Opposition by the Umayya family led to civil war from which the Umayyads emerged victorious. Ali was murdered, his supporters represent the beginning of the Shi'ite movement.

The Umayyad Caliphate (A.D. 661-750)

Ruled from Damascus. Among the Umayyad caliphs were Abd el-Malik (685-705) who built the "Dome of the Rock," al-Walid (705-715) who built the al-Aksa Mosque, Suleiman (715-717) who built Ramla and made it the chief administrative center for the Holy Land during the Early Arab period, and Hisham (724-743) who built the "Hisham Palace" at Jericho. al-Walid and Suleiman were sons of Abd el-Malik.

The Abbasid Caliphate (A.D. 750-969)

Ruled from Baghdad. This period represents a high point of Arab cultural achievement. Among the Abbasid caliphs was Harun ar-Rashid (786-809), the caliph of the "Thousand and One Nights."

The Fatimid Caliphate (969-1171)

A Shi'ite dynasty which established itself in Egypt, built Cairo as its capital, and gained an upper hand in the Holy Land and Syria. The Abbasids continued to rule in Baghdad.

The Ayyubid Caliphate (A.D. 1171-1266)

A dynasty established by Saladin in Egypt and Damascus. The Ayyubids in Damascus were overrun by the Mongols in 1260, the Ayyubids in Egypt having been displaced by the Mamluks in 1250.

CRUSADER KINGDOM OF JERUSALEM

The Crusaders established a kingdom in the Holy Land, with Jerusalem as the capital, which lasted about a hundred years—from the First Crusade in 1099 to Saladin's devastating defeat of a combined Crusader army at Hattin in 1187.

Godfrey of Bouillon (1099-1100)	Elected "Defender of the Holy Sepulchre." Defeated a Fatimid (Egyptian) army near Ashkelon.
Baldwin I (1100-1118)	Took the title "King" and extended the Crusader kingdom of Jerusalem to include virtually all of the Holy Land and southern Lebanon (but not the cities of Tyre and Ashkelon on the coast). Baldwin built the castle Montreal (present-day Shaubak) to defend his grip on southern Transjordan, possession of which allowed him to command the caravan route between Syria and Egypt. Also he built the castle Habis near the Yarmuk River and forced the Turkish ruler in Damascus to acknowledge his condominium over the territory east of the Sea of Galilee (the "Land of the Suhite").
Baldwin II (1118-1131)	Took Tyre from Egypt.
Fulk (1131-1144)	Constructed a line of castles along the northeastern frontier of his kingdom, a ring of castles around Ashkelon which was still in Egyptian hands, and the famous castle Le-Crac (present-day Kerak) in southern Transjordan. Military orders such as the Templars and the Hospitalers began to take responsibility for the security of Christian pilgrim routes.
Baldwin III (1144-1162)	Built a castle at Gaza and conquered Ashkelon (1153). The Crusader kingdom of Edessa fell to Zanki, a Turkish prince from Mosul, and a Second Crusade was undertaken in response (1144-1148). This Second Crusade did not achieve its goal. Moreover, Zanki's successor, Nur ad-Din, conquered Damascus in 1154 and began to threaten Baldwin's northeastern frontier.
Amalric (1162-1173)	Attempted with Byzantine support to conquer Egypt which was ruled now by exceedingly inept Fatimid caliphs. Nur ad-Din sent emissaries to organize resistance, among them being a Kurdish officer called Salah ad-Din (Saladin). The Crusaders withdrew in 1169 and Saladin declared the Fatimid caliphate ended in 1171.
Baldwin IV (1173-1185)	Already in control in Egypt, Saladin usurped control of Damascus at Nur ad-Din's death (1174) and within two years ruled all of Syria except Aleppo. Eventually he conquered Aleppo as well. Saladin now posed a serious threat to Baldwin's kingdom. The Crusader hold on southern Transjordan was especially problematic for Saladin, on the other hand, since the main caravan and pilgrimage routes from Syria to Egypt and Mecca passed through this area. The castles of Le-Crac (Kerak) and Montreal (Shaubak) became especially strategic.

THE LATER CRUSADES

A dispute regarding the succession to the throne following Baldwin IV's death remained unsettled in 1187 when Saladin defeated a combined Crusader army at the Horns of Hattin. This was a devastating blow. Virtually every fighting man the Crusaders could muster was killed or captured at Hattin. Saladin was now master of the Holy Land and within a year he held Jerusalem and all the coastal cities except Tyre.

The Third through the Eighth Crusades were undertaken following Saladin's victory at Hattin in an effort to restore the Crusader kingdom of Jerusalem. This was never accomplished.

Third Crusade (1190-1192)	Led by Frederick Barbarossa of Germany (who drowned on the way), Richard the Lionhearted (who stopped along the way to conquer Cyprus and arrived late) and Philip Augustus of France. They recovered Acre in 1191, then Ashkelon and Jaffa. Richard won a major victory over Saladin at Arsuf (in the Shephelah), but later had to give up Ashkelon to Saladin and was hard-pressed to defend Acre. Saladin died in 1193. Richard departed to England soon after with the Crusaders still in possession of the coast from Tyre to Jaffa. Acre has replaced Jerusalem as the Crusader capital.
Fourth Crusade (1202-1204)	Spent itself on the conquest of Byzantium and never reached the Holy Land.
Fifth Crusade (1217)	Hungarians and Germans; invaded Egypt with no permanent result.
Sixth Crusade (1228)	Saladin's united Syro-Egyptian state did not last long under his successors, the Ayyubids. Egypt remained strong, but Syria broke up into several smaller states. Since the Ayyubids were weakened by disunity, the leaders of the next two Crusades were able to achieve some success through peaceful negotiations. Thus Frederick II of Germany, who led the Sixth Crusade, secured Christian control of Jerusalem, Bethlehem and Nazareth, as well as a corridor from Jaffa to Jerusalem.
Seventh Crusade (1241-1244)	Thibant of Champagne persuaded an Ayyubid sultan of Damascus to cede more territory. Also, with Damascus' help, he recovered Ashkelon from the Ayyubid sultan of Cairo.
Eighth Crusade (1249-1254)	In 1244, just as it appeared that they might be able to make a comeback because of Ayyubid disunity, the Crusader forces were almost completely annhilated near Gaza by a horde of Khwarizmian Turks, whom the Ayyubid sultan of Egypt had called upon for help. The Eighth Crusade, led by Louis the Pious (St. Louis) of France, was in response to this near disaster. Louis attempted unsuccessfully to invade Egypt in 1249. Later he recovered some of the lost territory in the Holy Land and refortified Acre, Caesarea and Jaffa.

A Mongol invasion was halted by the Mamluks at Ain Jalud in 1260. Thereafter the Mamluks set about to reduce the remaining Crusader castles and to expel the Crusaders from the Holy Land once and for all. The last shipload of Crusader refugees departed Acre in 1291.

IMPORTANT DATES, PEOPLE AND EVENTS FROM THE MAMLUK PERIOD

The Mamluks were a powrful military caste, slaves in origin, who displaced the Ayyubids in Egypt and for two and a half centuries ruled an extended empire which included the Holy Land (1250-1516). The following are some important dates, people, and events from the Mamluk period.

1260   Baybars proclaimed himself sultan of Egypt, beginning the Bahrite line of Mamluk rulers. Three early sultans of this line—Baybars (1260-1277), Qalawun (1279-1290) and el-Ashraf Khalil (1290-1293)—reduced the remaining Crusader castles and expelled the last remnants of the Crusaders from the Holy Land.

1271   Marco Polo landed in Haifa in route to China.

1382   Bahrite line of Mamluk sultans replaced by Burjite (Circassian) line.

1400   Tamberlane invaded Syria and conquered Damascus. The Mamluks temporarily retreated from the Holy Land but returned in 1405 after Tamberlane's death.

1453   Byzantium/Constantinople fell to the Ottoman (Othman) Turks, under whom it came to be called Istanbul.

1480-1483   Felix Fabri made two pilgrimages to the Holy Land.

1492-1496   Jews expelled from Spain and Portugal. Many immigrated to the Holy Land.

IMPORTANT DATES, PEOPLE, AND EVENTS FROM THE OTTOMAN PERIOD

The Holy Land was, for four centuries, part of a vast Ottoman empire. Many of the archaeological discoveries which shed light on ancient Israel and her neighboring nations occurred during the last century of the Ottoman period.

1516   Ottoman Turks defeated a Mamluk army at Marj Dabiq.

1520-1566   The Ottoman empire reached its zenith during the reign of Sulieman "the Magnificent," extending from the outskirts of Vienna to the south-eastern tip of Arabia. Among his many accomplishments, Sulieman built the walls which surround the "Old City" of Jerusalem. The French gained special privileges in the Turkish empire (called "Capitulations") and assumed protectorate status over certain Christian sacred places in the Holy Land.

1590-1635   Fakreddin, a Druse leader, carved out an independent kingdom in southern Lebanon and upper Galilee.

1745-1775   Daher el-Omar ruled an independent kingdom centered at Acre.

1761   Karsten Niebuhr's travels in the Middle East.

1798-1801   Napoleon invaded Egypt and the Holy Land, but was halted at Acre, ruled at the time by Ahmed al-Jazzar. Napoleon's soldiers discovered the Rosetta Stone.

1804-1849   Mohammed Ali governed Egypt, supposedly as a viceroy of the Ottoman sultan, but in fact as an independent ruler who became a serious threat to the Ottoman empire. He brought Mamluk influence to an end in Egypt and, in 1818, waged a successful campaign against the Wahabis (which extended his domain to include northern Arabia). Another campaign in 1831, led by his son Ibrahim, added the Holy Land and much of Syria to Mohammed Ali's realm. The European powers forced Ibrahim to withdraw from the latter territories in 1840. Other important events contemporary with Mohammed Ali's reign were as follows:

1812 - Burkhardt discovered Petra.

1821 - Greece gained independence from the Ottoman empire.

1822 - Champollion deciphered Egyptian hieroglyphics.

1837 - Rawlinson made a copy of the Behistun Inscription. He deciphered the Persian column in 1846 and the Akkadian column soon after.

1838 - Robinson made his first visit to the Holy Land.

1842 - Lepsius conducterd a systematic survey of Egyptian inscriptions.

1853-1856   Crimean War. Among the contributing causes was a dispute between the Roman Catholic and the Greek (Byzantine) Orthodox priests at the Church of the Nativity.

1868   Mesha Inscription discovered.

1869   Suez Canal completed.

1872   George Adam Smith discovered a "Flood Story" among the cuneiform tablets excavated at Nineveh.

1872-1878   Palestine Exploration Fund sponsored a systematic mapping and archaeological survey of the area west of the Jordan River.

1877-1878   Russo-Turkish War. Circassian refugees from the Black Sea area were resettled in the Transjordan.

1878   Petah-Tikvah founded, the first modern Jewish settlement in the Holy Land.

1880   First Aliya (wave of Jewish immigration to the Holy Land). Siloam Inscription discovered.

1887   Amarna Letters discovered.

1890   Flinders Petrie began excavations at Tell el-Hesi. This was the first "tell" to be excavated in the Holy Land. Other tells excavated before World War I included Gezer, Beth-Shemesh, Megiddo, Taanach, Jericho and Samaria.

1897   First Zionist Congress held in Basel, Switzerland.

1898   Kaiser Wilhelm II of Germany visited the Holy Land. A breach was made in the Jerusalem wall, between the citadel and the Jaffa gate, for his grand entrance.

1904   Second Aliya.

1908   Hajaz railroad completed, connecting Damascus with Mecca.

1914-1918   World War I.

THE MIDDLE EAST DURING WORLD WAR I

1914   Outbreak of the war. England declared Egypt a protectorate and, with this as a base of operations, began the war effort against the Turks in the Middle East.

1915   Letters exchanged between Sir Henry McMahon, the British High Commissioner for Egypt and the Sudan, and Hussein Ibn Ali, Sharif of Mecca. It was agreed that Hussein and his four sons (Ali, Faisal, Abdullah, Zaid) would lead an Arab uprising against the Turks and that the British in turn would recognize and support the independence of the Arabs in their own lands. (There were some unresolved differences regarding the application of this agreement to the Mediterranean coastal region which had been under increasing French influence during the preceding century).

1916   Confidential diplomatic notes exchanged between Britain, France and Russia, known as the *Sykes-Picot Agreement*. This agreement anticipated the division of the territory of the Ottoman empire among the three nations involved and recognized France's claim to most of Syria. Syria, as understood in this context, would have included what is today Lebanon as well as part of the Holy Land.

1917   Arthur James Balfour, British Secretary of State for Foreign Affairs, indicated on November 2 in an official letter to Lord Rothschild that England favored the establishment in Palestine of a national home for the Jewish people. This came to be called the *Balfour Declaration*. Meanwhile, the Arab uprising, involving "Lawrence of Arabia," was well under way. An Arab army captured the port of Aqaba in July. From Egypt, General Allenby reached Jerusalem in December with a British army.

1918   The Arab army continued to push north through the Transjordan and took Damascus in October. The British reached Damascus three days later, but Allenby assumed command of the city in his capacity as head of the Allied Army of Emancipation. The concept of Arab independence was reconfirmed the following month by a joint Anglo-French declaration defining Allied war aims in the Middle East. The declaration promised "administrations deriving their authority from the initiative and free choice of the indigenous populations in Syria and Mesopotamia."

POLITICAL DEVELOPMENTS IN THE HOLY LAND FOLLOWING WORLD WAR I

1920   Mandate divisions worked out at the Peace Conference of San Remo (approved by the League of Nations in 1922). Britain received the Holy Land and Mesopotamia as mandates.

1921   Britain divided the Holy Land into two parts: the area west of the Jordan was designated "Palestine" to be administered directly by the British; the area east of the Jordan was designated an emirate (kingdom).

Abdullah, one of Sharif Hussein's sons who had marched north into the Transjordan with a Bedouin army, was appointed as first emir (king).

1923 Britain recognized the independence of the Emirate of Transjordan but kept unlimited rights to maintain military bases, thus remaining suzerain.

1930-1940 Jewish immigration to Palestine had begun to make a noticeable change in the population balance by the mid-1930's. Numerous acts of violence between Jews and Arabs.

1941-1945 World War II

1946 Britain, prompted by the loyalty of the Emirate of Transjordan during the war, recognized the kingdom as independent.

1947 On November 29 the United Nations passed a resolution favoring the establishment of a Jewish state in Palestine. The British gave notice that their mandate goverment would be terminated on May 14, 1948.

1948-1949 British mandate terminated; Israel proclaimed itself a nation; first Arab-Israeli war.

1951 Abdullah assassinated in al-Aksa Mosque and succeeded by his son Talal. Talal, unable to rule because of illness, was succeeded by his son, Hussein, in 1952.

1956 Egypt nationalized the Suez Canal. Second Arab-Israeli war. Israel invaded Gaza and Sinai during the war but withdrew under pressure from the United Nations.

1967 Third Arab-Israeli war, the so-called "Six-Day War." Israel occupied all of the territory west of the Jordan River, plus the Sinai and the Golan Heights.

1973 Fourth Arab-Israeli war, the so-called "Yom Kippur War."

1978 Israel invaded southern Lebanon.

1980 Camp David Accord.

1982 Israeli invasion of Lebanon.

Glossary of Geographical Terms
from Biblical Times

The following are some of the key geographical terms used during biblical times. Consult Maps 4-10 above.

Aijalon—A valley northwest of Jerusalem providing access to the hill country from the Shephelah. It was in connection with a battle fought in the Aijalon that Joshua commanded the sun to stand still (Joshua 10:12-13).

Ammon—The land of the Ammonites, surrounding and including Rabbah, their chief city. Rabbah (present-day Amman) was situated on a southeastern branch of the Jabbok River, between Gilead and the desert.

Arabah—The "Ghor" in Arabic. Generally, any part of the geological rift which extends from the Sea of Chinnereth (Galilee) down the course of the Jordan River to "the Sea of the Arabah" (the Dead Sea) and beyond to the Gulf of Aqaba. In the Old Testament Arabah sometimes refers specifically to that portion of the rift south of the Dead Sea.

Arnon River—Today called Wady el-Mujib, the Arnon river descends 3500 feet through a 30 mile long, steep-sided, narrow and deep gorge, and flows into the Dead Sea at the midpoint of its eastern shore. The Arnon marked the southern limit of ancient Israel's territorial claims in the Transjordan (Joshua 12:1-2; 13:9, 16).

Bashan—The rich pasture land east of the Sea of Chinnereth (Galilee) and the sources of the Jordan. Includes the Yarmuk River basin and the territory stretching northward to Mount Hermon (Joshua 9:10; 12:4-5; 13:1-12).

Brook of Egypt—Wady el-Arish, which enters the Mediterranean Sea at el-Arish, was called the Brook of Egypt during Old Testament times. As the biblical name suggests, the territory southwest of this brook (the Sinai Peninsula) was considered a part of Egypt.

Central Hill Country—The mountainous spine between the coastal plain on the west and the Jordan River Valley on the east and extending from the Jezreel Valley in the north to the Negeb in the south. The northern part of this central hill country (from Jezreel to approximately Jerusalem) was the tribal territory of Manasseh, Ephraim and Benjamin during Old Testament times and often referred to as the Ephraimite hill country. The southern part (from approximately Jerusalem to the Negeb) was the tribal territory of Judah and called the Judean hill country. During New Testament times these two parts of the central hill country were called Samaria and Judea respectively.

Dead Sea—The Jordan River empties into this lake which is the lowest spot in the world (1,240 feet = 378 m. below sea level). Forty-three miles long and nine miles wide, it also contains the most salt-saturated water in the world (approximately 25% salt and other minerals). "Dead Sea" is a fairly recent name. During Old Testament times it was called the Sea of Salt (Genesis 14:3; Numbers 34:3) or the Sea of the Arabah (Deuteronomy 4:49; Joshua 3:16). Classical geographers called it Lake Asphaltitis.

Decapolis—The name means "ten cities" in Greek and referred to a confederation of approximately ten cities which was formed following Pompey's invasion of Syria-Palestine in 64 B.C. As a geographical term, Decapolis referred to the northern Transjordan where these cities were clustered (Matthew 4:25). All but one of the Decapolis cities, Scythopolis (the Beth Shean of Old Testament times; present-day Bet She'an), were situated east of the Jordan rift. Also comprising the confederation were Damascus, Gadara (present-day Um Qeis), Gerasa (Jerash) and Philadelphia (Rabbah of the Ammonites in Old Testament times; present-day Amman).

Edom—Land of the Edomites during Old Testament times; south of the Zered River. This area was dominated by the Nabateans during New Testament times and called Nabatea.

Ephraimite Hill Country—That portion of the central hill country approximately between Jerusalem and Shechem. In New Testament times this area and northward to the Jezreel (Esdraelon) Valley was called Samaria.

Esdraelon Valley—See "Jezreel Valley."

Galilee—During New Testament times the mountainous area north of Jezreel (Esdraelon) and west of the Sea of Chinnereth/Galilee was called Galilee. Nazareth is situated in the southern foothills of Galilee.

Gennesaret—A pleasant, fertile plain along the northwestern shore of the Sea of Galilee (Matthew 14:34; Mark 6:53).

Gilead—The mountainous area east of the Jordan, bisected by the Jabbok River (Joshua 12:2, 5; 13:11, 25, 31; 17:1).

Idumea—After Jerusalem was conquered by the Babylonians in the sixth century B.C. Edomites appear to have gained possession of the southern part of the central hill country south of Hebron. Thus this area came to be called Idumea, "the land of the Edomites."

Jabbok River—A large tributary of the Jordan that drops 3200 feet while cutting through the mountainous region of Gilead. According to Joshua 12:2, it marked the northern limits of Sihon's kingdom. Called Nahr ez-Zerqa today.

Jezreel Valley—The valley which separates Galilee from Mount Carmel and the central hill country. The name is appropriate in referring more specifically to that portion of the valley immediate to the Old Testament village of Jezreel. The Greek pronunciation of Jezreel, in use during New Testament times, is "Esdraelon."

Jordan River—The river beginning at the foot of Mount Hermon and flowing into the Dead Sea.

Judean Hill Country—That part of the central hill country south of Jerusalem; core of the kingdom of Judah during Old Testament times and later of the Roman province of Judea.

Judean Wilderness—The barren eastern slopes of the southern (Judean) part of the central hill country. Throughout history this has served as sanctuary for outlaws, rebels and religious idealists.

Kishon River—Drains the western Jezreel Valley into the Mediterranean Sea at present-day Haifa. According to Judges 4:7, Israel's armies, led by Barak and Deborah, defeated Sisera near the Kishon.

Litani River—Drains the southern end of the valley between the Lebanon and Anti-Lebanon Mountains.

Moab—The plateau area directly east of the Dead Sea; land of the Moabites during Old Testament times; bisected by the Arnon River.

Mount Carmel—This northwestern spur of the central hill country extends into the Mediterranean Sea immediately south of Acre.

Mount Ebal—Mounts Ebal and Gerizim are two prominent heights overlooking a pass through the central hill country at the site of ancient Shechem. Mount Ebal is situated on the north, Gerizim on the south, and the "tell" of ancient Shechem in between (Joshua 8:30, 33).

Mount Gerizim—See Mount Ebal.

Mount Gilboa—A spur of the central hill country which juts into the Jezreel

Valley not far from the Jordan River. Saul and Jonathan fell in battle on Mount Gilboa (1 Samuel 28-31).

Mount Hermon—The tallest (about 9000 feet) and southernmost spur of the Anti-Lebanon range (Joshua 11:3, 17; 12:1, 5; 13:5, 11).

Mount Nebo—See Pisgah.

Mount Pisgah—See Pisgah.

Mount Tabor—A solitary hill (about 1700 feet) in the Jezreel Valley. The tribes of Zebulun, Issachar and Naphtali may have had a common sanctuary on Mount Tabor during Old Testament times (see Joshua 19:22, 34). According to one tradition, this was the "Mount of Transfiguration" (Matthew 17:1-13; Mark 9:2-13).

Mount Zion—One of the mountain ridges on which the city of Jerusalem is situated.

Nabatea—Historians are uncertain of the origin and early history of the Nabateans. References to them began to appear in written records during the Hellenistic period. By New Testament times they had established a commercial empire based at Petra and were in control of southern Transjordan. Accordingly, this area was called Nabatea.

Negeb—The "dry land" area south of Beersheba, extending from the Gulf of Aqaba to Gaza. This area is mountainous in the central and southern parts, with deep valleys.

Perea—"Beyond" in Greek; refers to the area immediately east of the Jordan river.

Philistine Plain—The southern coastal plain inhabited by the Philistines. Classical geographers called it "Philistia," from which the term Palestine is derived.

Pisgah—The name can refer to either a section of the mountains of Abarim overlooking the northeastern shores of the Dead Sea or to a particular promontory of that range. Sihon's kingdom is recorded to have extended as far as the eastern side of the Sea of the Arabah below "the slopes of Pisgah" (Joshua 12:3), and Moses is said to have viewed the promised land from Pisgah (Deuteronomy 3:27). Mount Pisgah and Mount Nebo may have been synonymous (Deuteronomy 32:49; 34:1).

Samaria—The New Testament name for the northern part of the central hill country. The name was derived from the city of Samaria, capital of the northern Israelite kingdom.

Sea of Chinnereth—Called the Sea of Galilee in the New Testament, this lake, 600 feet below sea level, is approximately 12 miles long and 5 miles wide.

"Chinnereth" is probably derived from a Naphtalian city of the same name which was situated on the seashore (Joshua 11:2; 12:3; 13:27, 19:35).

Sea of Galilee—See Sea of Chinnereth.

Sharon Plain—The northern part of the coastal plain. The name Sharon probably meant "plain" or "level country" in ancient Hebrew.

Shephelah—The "foothills" which lie between the coastal (Philistine) plain and the Judean hill country.

Yarmuk River—Drains Bashan and empties into the Jordan River immediately south of the Sea of Chinnereth (Galilee). The Yarmuk is not mentioned in the Bible.

Zared River—Called Wady el-Hesa today, this river canyon served as a natural boundary between Moab and Edom during ancient times.

More about Jerusalem

On any trip to the Holy Land the city of Jerusalem is sure to be the high point. This is due to its fascinating history, the religious implications which the "City of David" carries in everyone's mind, and the deep significance this ancient city has in world events of today. A question that naturally arises in a Christian's mind is, "What was Jerusalem like in Jesus' day?" Certainly it did not look then as it does now.

Summary of Jerusalem's History Through the Ages. Jerusalem was already a very old city when it fell into Israelite hands. It is mentioned in Egyptian texts from the Bronze Age, for example, and one of these texts refers to a pre-Israelite king of Jerusalem named Abdu-Heba (see "Letter from Abdu-Heba of Jerusalem," above, under "Deciphering Ancient Languages"). Genesis 14:17-21 describes an occasion when Abraham paid tribute to one "Melchizedek of Salem." "Salem" possibly is an abbreviated form of "Jerusalem." Archaeological investigations indicate that Bronze Age Jerusalem was confined to Ophel (see "Ophel," above, under "Jerusalem and Vicinity").

David conquered Jerusalem approximately 1000 B.C. and made it the capital of his kingdom (2 Samuel 5:6-7). Solomon expanded the city, building a palace and temple apparently in the area where the Dome of the Rock monument stands today (1 Kings 5-8). When the Israelite monarchy was divided into two kingdoms after Solomon's death (1 Kings 12), Jerusalem continued as the capital of the southern kingdom, Judah. A list of the Judean kings is provided in the chronological chart above.

Jerusalem was destroyed by the Babylonians in 586 B.C. (2 Kings 25), but a small struggling Jewish community endured in the city for another 400 years, dominated in turn by the Babylonians, the Persians, the Ptolemys and the Seleucids. The book of Lamentations reflects the situation in Jerusalem soon after its fall to the Babylonians, while the books of Ezra and Nehemiah record developments during the Persian period. For information about Jerusalem under the Ptolemys and Seleucids, historians must depend heavily on Josephus, a Jewish historian who lived during the first century A.D.

Ca. 166 B.C. Judas Maccabeus led the Jews in rebellion against the Seleucid ruler Antiochus IV. The rebellion was successful and an independent Jewish dynasty was established which would rule in Jerusalem for the next 100 years. This is called the "Hasmonean" dynasty after Judas' family name, and the century of their rule is called the "Maccabean" period. I Maccabees provides an account of the rebellion. A list of the Hasmonean rulers is found in the chronological chart above. Jerusalem was expanded considerably during the Maccabean period.

Jerusalem was dominated by the Romans from 63 B.C., when Pompey marched against the city to settle a dispute between two Hasmonean claimants to the throne, until the fourth century A.D., when the center of eastern political affairs shifted to Byzantium/Constantinople. Herod the Great (37-4 B.C.), who was by far the most famous ruler of Jerusalem under the Romans, undertook an extensive building program. It is essentially Herod's Jerusalem which Jesus would have known. The city was modified and badly damaged as a result of the following events during the first and second centuries A.D.:

- Herod Agrippa (A.D. 37-44) expanded Jerusalem and built a third wall north of the previous fortifications.
- Titus conquered Jerusalem, destroying the Temple and much of the city in connection with the First Jewish Revolt (A.D. 66-70).
- Hadrian put down a second Jewish revolt (the Bar-Kochba Revolt) in A.D. 135, redesigned the city, and renamed it Aelia Capitolina. ("Aelia" refers to Hadrian's family name, "Aelius"; "Capitolina" refers to the Roman god Jupiter, also known as "Capitolinus.") Hadrian expelled the Jews from Jerusalem, cleared the temple area, and erected a statue to Jupiter where the temple had stood. Jerusalem became essentially a pagan city thereafter.

Jerusalem fell increasingly within the political realm of Byzantium, especially during and following the reign of Constantine in the fourth century. Christianity soon became the official state religion of the whole Roman-Byzantine world. Churches sprang up throughout the Holy Land marking the spots where various New Testament events were thought to have occurred. Among the churches founded in Jerusalem at that time were the Church of the Holy Sepulchre and the Church of the Crucifixion (not yet under a single roof).

Conquered by Caliph Omar in A.D. 637, Jerusalem remained in Arab hands until it was taken by Seljuk Turks in 1077. Moslems honor the Jewish prophets, including among them Jesus. But more important, they believe that the rock outcropping in the temple area at Jerusalem is actually "el-aksa" ("the distant place") where Mohammad was carried on his famous Night Journey and from which he received a vision of paradise. As early as the seventh century, therefore, Caliph Abd el-Malik built a monument (the so-called "Dome of the Rock") over this rock outcropping. His son, al-Walid, built the al-Aksa Mosque nearby. The Arabic name for Jerusalem is el-Quds, which means "the Holy Place."

The Crusaders took Jerusalem from the Seljuk Turks in 1099 and made it the center of a kingdom, having all the characteristics of a medieval European principality (castles, lords, ladies, knights and all). This kingdom lasted for approximately 100 years, until 1187, when Saladin routed the Crusaders' army at the Horns of Hattin. Saladin took Jerusalem later that same year. During the Crusader period, Jerusalem was again under Christian domination although this time it was the Roman Catholic (Latin rite) branch which had the upper hand rather than the Orthodox, or Byzantine (Greek rite) branch. The city witnessed a new phase of church building.

Jerusalem was dominated and exploited by Mamluk rulers from Egypt for approximately three centuries following the Crusader period. Then, in 1517, it fell to the Ottoman Turks and remained a city of the Ottoman empire until "liberated" by Allenby during World War I. The walls which surround the Old City today were built by the famous Ottoman sultan, Suleiman the Magnificent, in 1537-1542. Many of the buildings inside these walls date from the Ottoman period as well. The expansion of Jerusalem beyond the Old City walls has, for the most part, occurred since World War I.

The partition of Israel in 1948 left Jerusalem a divided city, which it remained until 1967. Jordan controlled the Old City (that part within the Turkish Walls) whose Arab population expanded to the north, east and south with new business and residential districts. Israel controlled the area west of the Old City wall and a large Jewish metropolis developed in that direction. Israel has held the Arab section of Jerusalem since the 1967 war.

Jerusalem as Jesus Knew It. Herod the Great lavishly remodeled the post-exilic Jewish temple, constructed a massive enclosure wall around the Temple area, erected a fort (the Antonia) at its northwest corner, erected three defensive towers at a particularly vulnerable point in the western city wall, and built a beautiful palace inside the city defenses. It was essentially this Jerusalem of Herod's day which witnessed Jesus' ministry. The model of Herodian Jerusalem at the Holy Land Hotel provides a good overview of the city plan at this stage, although one must keep in mind that the model includes a third (northern) city wall which was added later by Herod Agrippa.

Christian pilgrims began to find their way to Jerusalem as early as the second century; during the Byzantine period (fourth through the sixth centuries) they flocked there by the hundreds. These pilgrims naturally wanted to know, as do Christian tourists today, exactly where in the city the various New Testament events occurred. The New Testament itself rarely provides specific information of this sort. Already by the beginning of the Byzantine period, however, traditions were circulating among Palestinian Christians purporting to identify the actual places and churches were being built to mark and commemorate the sacred spots. The approximate locations of many of these early Byzantine churches are still known today.

Regarding the authenticity of these "traditional" New Testament sites, therefore, the issue usually is not whether Christians even as early as the fourth century believed them to be the actual places where the various New Testament events occurred, but whether these Christians themselves really knew. Most of the traditions in question cannot be traced back any further than the fourth century, which leaves a time gap of approximately 250 years between the crucifixion and the founding of the earliest Byzantine churches. During this 250 years Jerusalem was devastated by the Romans and rebuilt as a pagan city; Jews were expelled and, at least for a time, the Christians fled to Pella (see above, under "Gilead, Bashan, and the Decapolis").

The real question is this: Do the early Christian traditions concerning the actual spots where New Testament events occurred represent authentic memory which survived the two and a half centuries that Jerusalem was essentially a pagan city? Or do they represent pious speculation on the part of the early Church in response to the natural curiosity of pilgrims who began to flock to the Holy Land after Christianity had received official recognition and begun to flourish? The debate goes on among scholars and the details of the debate vary depending on the site in question. The following are some of the traditional spots in Jerusalem which deserve special mention:

- **The Pool of Siloam.** According to John 9:1-12, Jesus healed a blind man with spit-clay and sent him to the Pool of Siloam to wash. This one we can be fairly certain about. The Pool of Siloam, situated on the southwestern slope of Ophil, is still in use (see above, under "Jerusalem and Vicinity").

- **The pool of Beth-zatha.** Also called Bethseda or Bethsaida, John 5:2-9 describes this as a pool with five porticoes, located near the Sheep Gate. The passage goes on to describe how Jesus healed a man who had been there for thirty-eight years, unable because of his illness to get into the pool quickly enough when the waters were troubled. Early pilgrims to Jerusalem spoke of the "twin pools" of Bethsaida. In 1888 workmen were clearing some ruins on the grounds of the St. Anne Church and discovered an old fresco which seems to represent the healing of the man at the pool. Excavations at the spot have revealed what could possibly be interpreted as the layout of a pool with porticoes.

- **The Garden of Gethsemane.** All four gospels record the incident of Jesus' agonizing prayer and betrayal by Judas. Matthew 26:36 and Mark 14:32 relate that the incident occurred in a "field" called Gethsemane (the name Gethsemane probably means "oil vat "). The other two gospels do not actually call the place by name: Luke 22:39-40 informs us only that the incident took place on the Mount of Olives; John 18:1-11 notes that it occurred "across the Kidron Valley" where there was a garden. Apparently Gethsemane (whether it was a field, garden, oil vat or whatever) was located on the Mount of Olives side of the Kidron. The beautiful garden pointed out today is as likely a spot as any. However, the claim that the roots of the olive trees in this garden are "very old, possibly dating back to the first century," has no bearing on the question of whether it is in fact the authentic Gethsemane.

- **The "Upper Room" and the House of Caiaphas.** Early Christian tradition located the site of the Upper Room (Mark 14:15; Luke 22:12) on Mount Zion. It was believed that the apostles celebrated the first Pentecost in this same room (Acts 1:13) and that Caiaphas' house was located nearby (Matthew 26:57; Mark 14:53; Luke 22:54). Thus a major church was erected on Mount Zion during the Byzantine Period and is depicted in the Madaba Mosaic Map (see above, under "The King's Highway to Petra," and Map 14). The idea that King David was buried in this vicinity is also a matter of unverified tradition. The complex of old buildings located on Mount Zion today date from medieval times and later. The "Cenacle," for example, which includes the traditional Upper Room and David's Tomb, is a fourteenth century restoration of a Crusader church.

- **The Church of the Holy Sepulchre.** Constantine commissioned the building of a church over what was believed at the time (A.D. 326) to be the place of Jesus' burial. This "Church of the Holy Sepulchre" has been the climax of Christian pilgrimages to the Holy Land for sixteen and a half centuries. The traditional site of the crucifixion (Golgotha) is nearby and has been included under the same roof with the Church of the Holy Sepulchre since the Crusader period. Serious doubts have been raised during modern times as to whether the Church of the Holy Sepulchre marks the actual sites of Jesus' crucifixion and burial, however, and an alternate candidate (the so-called "Garden tomb") is very popular among Protestant tourists. The crucial arguments on both sides of the question are as follows:

Supporting the "Garden tomb" as the authentic site:
> (1) It may well be that by the fourth century, when Constantine commissioned the Church of the Holy Sepulchre, Christians no longer remembered the exact place of Jesus' burial. In other words, the location of the Church may be based on pious speculation rather than on actual memory.

(2) There is some reason to believe, in fact, that the place where the Church of the Holy Sepulchre stands would have been inside the city walls during Jesus' day. Yet the crucifixion and burial would have occurred outside the city walls. Actually the exact position of the walls during the Roman period cannot be established with certainty, but in any case the Garden tomb would have been outside.

(3) The Garden tomb is near a rock cliff which, if one uses a bit of imagination, does look something like a skull (see Matthew 27:33; Mark 15:22).

Supporting the Church of the Holy Sepulchre as the authentic site:

(1) It is at least possible that the Christians of the fourth century did remember the exact spots of the crucifixion and burial, and in any case they were much nearer in time to these events than we are today. No known early traditions point to the Garden Tomb.

(2) The skull-like features of the rock cliff near the Garden tomb are the result of depressions left by cisterns dug into the rock from above and later broken away. This may have been a fairly recent development. These depressions are not noticeable in a seventeenth century drawing of the cliff.

(3) It is questionable whether the Garden tomb itself actually dates back to New Testament times. Moreover, it seems to have had a door at the entrance rather than a rolling stone. The rock-cut trough in front of the entrance almost certainly was intended for water drainage.

The fact is, we *really do not know* where the tomb or Golgotha was located.

Constantine Commissions the Church of the Holy Sepulchre

The Church of the Holy Sepulchre was commissioned by Emperor Constantine immediately following the Council of Nicea (A.D. 325). According to Eusebius, Bishop of Caesarea who participated in the Council and served as consultant to Constantine, Jesus' tomb had been covered with soil, paved, and desecrated with a temple to Venus.

> This sacred cave, then, certain impious and godless persons had thought to remove entirely from the eyes of men, supposing in their folly that thus they should be able effectually to obscure the truth. Accordingly they brought a quantity of earth from a distance with much labor, and covered the entire spot; then, having raised this to a

moderate height, they paved it with stone, concealing the holy cave beneath this massive mound.

Then, as though their purpose had been effectually accomplished, they prepared on this foundation a truly dreadful sepulchre of souls, by building a gloomy shrine of lifeless idols to the impure spirit whom they call Venus, and offering detestable oblations therein on profane and accused altars.

Eusebius' account continues, describing how, at Constantine's command, the pagan temple was demolished and even the polluted soil was transported to a far distance.

This also was accomplished without delay. But as soon as the original surface of the ground, beneath the covering of earth, appeared, immediately, and contrary to all expectations, the venerable and hallowed monument of our Savior's resurrection was discovered. . . . Immediately after the transactions I have recorded, the emperor sent forth injunctions which breathed a truly pious spirit, at the same time granting ample supplies of money, and commanding that a house of prayer worthy of worship of God should be erected near the Savior's tomb on a scale of rich royal greatness.
(*Life of Constantine* Book III, chs. 25-28)

Somewhat later there arose a tradition that Helena, Constantine's mother, had been involved in the discovery of the tomb, and that she had actually found the "true cross" in a cistern nearby. Her discovery of the cross is first mentioned by St. Ambrose in A.D. 395.

Suggestions for Further Reading

The Holy Land in Context
(General works on the peoples and empires of the ancient Middle East)

Aldred, C. *The Egyptians*. New York: Frederick A. Praeger, 1966.

Burney, C. *The Ancient Near East*. Ithaca, N.Y.: Cornell University, 1977.

David, Rosalie A. *The Egyptian Kingdoms*. New York: E. P. Dutton, 1975.

Ermar, A., editor. *The Ancient Egyptians*. New York: Harper and Row, 1966.

Frye, R. N. *The Heritage of Persia*. New York: New American Library, 1963.

Gray, John. *The Canaanites*. London: Thames and Hudson, 1964.

Gurney, O. R. *The Hittites*. Baltimore: Penguin Books, 1966.

Hallo, W. W. and Simpson, W. K. *The Ancient Near East: A History*. New York: Harcourt Brace Jovanovich, 1971.

Hawkes, Jacquetta. *The First Civilizations: Life in Mesopotamia, the Indus Valley, and Egypt*. New York: Alfred A. Knopf, 1973.

Moscati, S. *The World of the Phoenicians*. London: Weidenfield and Nicholson, 1968.

Olmstead, A. T. *History of the Persian Empire*. Chicago: The University of Chicago Press, 1948.

Oppenheim, A. L. *Ancient Mesopotamia*. Chicago: University of Chicago Press, 1964.

Saggs, H. W. F. *The Greatness that was Babylon*. New York: New American Library, Inc. 1962.

Steindorff, G. and Seele, K. C. *When Egypt Ruled the East*. Chicago: University of Chicago Press, 1957.

Wiseman, D. J., editor. *Peoples of Old Testament Times*. Oxford: Clarendon Press, 1973.

Wright, G. E., editor. *The Bible and the Ancient Near East*. Garden City, N.Y.: Doubleday & Co., 1961.

Rediscovering the Ancient World
(Works on archaeology of the Middle East and translations of ancient documents)

Ceram, C. W. *Gods, Graves, and Scholars*. London: Sidgwick & Jackson, 1951.

_____ . *The Secret of the Hittites: The Discovery of an Ancient Empire*. New York: Schocken Books, 1973.

Coogan, M. D., editor. *Stories from Ancient Canaan*. Philadelphia: Westminster Press, 1978.

Finley, M. I. *Atlas of Classical Archaeology*. London: Chatto & Windus, 1977.

Hawkes, Jacquetta, editor. *Atlas of Ancient Archaeology*. London: Heinemann, 1974.

Lloyd, Seton. *Foundations in the Dust*. Baltimore: Penguin Books, 1955.

_____ . *The Archaeology of Mesopotamia, From the Old Stone Age to the Persian Conquest*. London: Thames and Hudson, 1978.

Pfeiffer, C. F., editor. *The Biblical World: A Dictionary of Biblical Archaeology*. Grand Rapids, Mich.: Baker Book House, 1966.

Pritchard, J. B., editor. *The Ancient Near East in Pictures*. Princeton: Princeton University Press, 1954.

_____ . *Ancient Near Eastern Texts Relating to the Old Testament*. Princeton: Princeton University Press, 1955.

_____ . *The Ancient Near East Supplement*. Princeton: Princeton University Press, 1969.

Thomas, D. W. *Documents from Old Testament Times*. New York: Harper Torchbooks, 1961.

Wilson, J. A. *Signs and Wonders upon Pharaoh: A History of American Egyptology*. Chicago: University of Chicago Press, 1964.

The Holy Land during Biblical Times
(General works on the geography and archaeology of Palestine as related to the Bible)

Aharoni, Y. *The Land of the Bible*. Philadelphia: Westminster Press, 1967.

Baly, D. *The Geography of the Bible*. New York: Harper & Row, revised ed., 1974.

Finegan, J. *The Archaeology of the New Testament*. Princeton, N.J.: Princeton University Press, 1970.

Frank, H. T. *Discovering the Biblical World*. New York: Harper & Row, 1975.

Grollenberg, L. H. *The Penguin's Shorter Atlas of the Bible*. Baltimore: Penguin Books, 1978.

Kenyon, K. M. *Archaeology in the Holy Land*. New York: W. W. Norton, and Co., 4th ed., 1979.

_____ . *The Bible in Recent Archaeology*. Atlanta: John Knox Press, 1979.

Lance, H. D. *The Old Testament and the Archaeologist*. Philadelphia: Fortress Press, 1981.

Lapp, N. L. *The Tale of a Tell*. Pittsburgh: Pickwick Press, 1975.

Lapp, P. W. *Biblical Archaeology and History*. Cleveland: World Publishing Co., 1969.

Magnusson, M. *BC: The Archaeology of the Bible Lands*. London: Bodley Head, 1977.

Miller, J. M. *The Old Testament and the Historian*. Philadelphia: Fortress Press, 1976.

Paul, S. M. and Dever, G. W. *Biblical Archaeology*. Jerusalem: Keter Publishing House, 1973.

Schoville, K. N. *Biblical Archaeology in Focus*. Grand Rapids: Baker Book House, 1978.

**Non-Technical Journals for
Biblical Archaeology**

The Biblical Archaeologist. Published quarterly by the American Schools of Oriental Research, 126 Inman Street, Cambridge, Mass. 02139.

The Biblical Archaeology Review. Published quarterly by the Biblical Archaeology Society, 1819 H Street, N.W., Washington, D.C. 20006.

Biblical Illustrator (formerly *Sunday School Lesson Illustrator*). Published by the Baptist Sunday School Board with focus on archaeology and other matters relevant to biblical studies. Very useful. Subscribe through Materials Services Department, 127 Ninth Avenue North, Nashville, Tennessee 37234.

Jerusalem

Bahat, D. *Carta's Historical Atlas of Jerusalem.* Jerusalem: Carta, 1973.

Gray, John. *A History of Jerusalem.* London: Robert Hale, 1969.

Kenyon, K. *Digging up Jerusalem.* New York: Praeger Publishing Company, 1974. Essentially the same as her *Jerusalem, Digging 3000 Years of History,* New York: McGraw-Hill, 1967.

Shamis, Giora and Shalem, Diane. *The Jerusalem Guide.* London: Abraham Marcus, Ltd., 1973.

Wilkinson, J. *Jerusalem as Jesus Knew It.* London: Thames and Hudson, 1978.

Yadin, Y., editor. *Jerusalem Revealed: Archaeology in the Holy City, 1968-1974.* Jerusalem: Israel Exploration Society, 1975.

Other Places of Special Interest

Browning, I. *Petra.* Park Ridge, N.J.: Noyes Press, 1973.

Kenyon, K. *Digging up Jericho.* New York: Praeger, 1957.

Pritchard, J. B. *Gibeon Where the Sun Stood Still.* Princeton: Princeton University Press, 1973.

Wright, G. E. *Shechem: The Biography of a Biblical City.* New York: McGraw-Hill, 1975.

Yadin, Y. *Masada.* New York: Random House, 1966.

———. *Hazor.* New York: Random House, 1975.

Guidebooks

Archaeology. Israel Pocket Library—articles on individual archaeological sites west of the Jordan, selected from *The Encyclopedia Judaica.*

Bozak Guide to Israel, 1980-1981. Jerusalem: Bazak Israel Guidebook Publishers, 1980; distributed by Harper & Row.

Hoade, Eugene, o.f.m. *Guide to the Holy Land.* Jerusalem: Franciscan Printing Press, ⁹1978.

———. *East of the Jordan.* Jerusalem: Franciscan Printing Press, 1966. Edited and republished by Fr. Claudio Barratto under the title *Guide to Jordan,* Franciscan Printing Press, 1978.

Lewensohn, A. *Israel Tourguide.* Tel Aviv: Tourguide, Ltd., ²1979.

O'Connor, Murphy J. *The Holy Land: An Archaeological Guide from Earliest Times to 1700*. New York: Oxford University Press, 1980.

Vilnay, Z. *The Guide to Israel*. Jerusalem: Hamakor Press, [13]1970.

The Dead Sea Scrolls

Cross, F. M. *The Ancient Library of Qumran and Modern Biblical Studies*. Garden City, N.Y.: Doubleday, 1961.

Dupont-Sommer, A. *The Essene Writings from Qumran*. Gloucester, Mass.: Peter Smith, 1961.

Vermes, G. *The Dead Sea Scrolls in English*. Baltimore: Penguin Books, 1972.

Yadin, Y. *Bar Kokhba*. New York: Random House, 1971.

Arabs and Israelis

Finegan, J. *Discovering Israel: A Popular Guide to the Holy Land*. Grand Rapids: Eerdmans, 1981.

Gibb, H. *Mohammadanism*. New York: Oxford University Press, 1968.

Levy, B. *The Middle East and West*. New York: Harper Torchbooks, 1964.

Mansfield, P. *The Arabs*. Gretna, La.: Pelican Paperback, 1978.

Sykes, C. *Crossroads to Israel*. Bloomington: Indiana University Press, 1973.

List of Maps

List of Photographs

Chronological Outlines

Non-Biblical Documents
Quoted in the Guidebook

Index

Places Included in the Itineraries